look
good
now

AND ALWAYS

a do-it-yourself
style makeover
for busy women

*To Abby,
Thanks for shining
your light in the
world!
Love,
Marian Rothschild*

by marian rothschild

Published in the United States by Confident Leadership Image, an imprint of Confident Leadership Press, CO.

Rothschild, Marian
Look Good Now and Always:
A do-it-yourself style makeover for busy women / Marian Rothschild

Includes quotes and references.

Printed in the United States of America on acid-free paper.

Visit our website at: www.marianrothschild.com

Cover and interior book design by Launie Parry, Red Letter Creative.

ISBN: 978-0-615-90156-5

To Mark, my ROK

Acknowledgements

Much gratitude goes out to all the many clients, advisors, colleagues, friends, loved ones, supporters, and anyone else who helped with the creation of this book in any way. I am deeply appreciative of all you've done for me, ever. Very special thanks go out to; Aimee Heckel Markwardt, Leslie Miller, Launie Parry, Lori DeBoer, Kim Huss, Marianne and Todd Ballantine, Barbara Wilson, Andy Mendoza, Sally Walker, Jacqueline Madrid, Vicki Goldstein, Nicole DeBoom, Colleen DeReuck, Kathy Sabine, Kim, Robin, J.D., Paige, Christina, Rosalind, Suzanne, Luke, Erik, Mark of course, my father Joe, the first in our family to write his story, and my first inspirations Kathy, Vanessa, and my loving mother Marjorie.

TABLE OF *Contents*

Introduction

Many people have asked how I got into the business of personal styling and image consulting. My own journey – spanning childhood challenges, the struggle to fit in, and then a life on stage – naturally culminated here. I learned as a child that a confident image and strong sense of personal style made it easier to fit into new situations, especially if unsure of the rules.

Picture this – a little third grade girl at Infant Jesus of Prague Catholic School in a southwestern suburb of Chicago. Our school uniform was a white blouse, red sweater, red and green tartan-plaid wool skirt with tiny one-inch pleats. Each one of those pleats had to be meticulously ironed. The only clothing option you had besides the school uniform, was if you were a Girl Scout or Brownie, you could wear your scout dress to school, but only on the day of your scout meeting.

One Monday morning, I reached in the closet for my school clothes and something was missing.

"Where's my skirt?"

I dashed down the hall to the laundry room, hoping to find my skirt hanging, ironed. Instead, I opened the washing machine and gasped. There, crumpled and wet at the bottom of the washer, was my school uniform skirt. The bus was minutes away. I grabbed the skirt and ran to my parents' room. The door was closed. That meant that my mother was still in bed, probably asleep, after having been up with my baby brother during the night.

I knocked. No answer. I knocked again louder. No answer.

"Mom, my skirt needs to be ironed! The bus is coming. Mom, you have to do this for me!" By this time tears were flowing. This was a catastrophe.

From the other side of the door came my mother's soft, gravelly voice, "Marian, just wear your Girl Scout dress to school today."

"I can't! Today's not my troop meeting!"

"Marian, just wear the scout dress, and I'll iron your skirt this afternoon."

I was devastated. That couldn't happen. The nuns had *rules* and stiff penalties for disobeying them. If I got caught wearing my scout dress on a day that I didn't have a meeting, there was no telling what might happen. At the tender age of eight, I couldn't stand the embarrassment resulting from being out of uniform.

I'd seen the nuns' anger and heard the stories of kids' hands being slapped with rulers – and worse.

But the bus was coming. Reluctantly I changed into the green scout dress, belt, and knee socks. I felt like a fraud, slipping the sash with the badges over my left shoulder, under my right arm... walking out to the bus stop... climbing the steps up onto the bus... taking my seat. I stared out the window, flooded with shame, embarrassment, and fear.

The memory of my humiliation in first grade was still fresh in my mind. Sister Elanita had made me fetch my older sister Vanessa from the fourth grade classroom. In front of my whole class, the nun told Vanessa to go home and tell my mother that I was stupid because I didn't know my murmur diphthongs.

Riding the bus to school that morning I worried that some catty girl would "innocently" announce, "Hey, you don't have Girl Scouts today!" And then all hell would break loose.

By mid-morning, my head ached. At lunch recess I shuffled around the playground by myself, head low, shoulders drooped, trying to avoid any conversation which might lead to someone finding out.

When the bell rang for 3:00 dismissal, I felt like I'd gotten away with murder. No one noticed I wore the wrong uniform. By the time I boarded the school bus, my head pounded from the stress of "defrauding" the institution my parents were counting on to save our souls.

My mother greeted me as I walked in the back door. "Your skirt is ironed," she said nonchalantly, as if it was no big deal. "It's right there. Go hang it in your closet."

I snatched the skirt. "Thank goodness! I never want to do that again," I yelled, slamming the bedroom door behind me.

I'm sure many of you can relate to this story, nuns or not. Even young girls and boys want to fit in appropriately, genuinely, and authentically. What we wear and how we present ourselves is integral to our concept of who we are, as well as how we're recognized and accepted by others. Our self-image, along with the image we want the world to see, is one of the things that define us. Personal style is one way to represent on the outside *who we are on the inside*.

If you don't think that matters to children, try negotiating with a three-year-old preschooler about what to wear for Halloween or a birthday party. It matters to *her*, and she will be *quite* insistent.

Fast-forward to the start of seventh grade. Glory hallelujah, I was off to Flossmoor Junior High, the local public school where you could wear whatever you wanted within the guidelines of a dress code. A whole new world opened up for me.

I was in school with my best friend, Kim Hercules. Her family belonged to the country club, her mother drove a Cadillac convertible, and they had a cleaning lady! They shopped at trendy teen boutiques and bought bell-bottoms, culottes, peasant blouses, and even white go-go boots – the epitome of fashion in those days. Kim had style, her parents had money, and to me that meant that she had it made. She didn't have to scrounge around to put a look together; she just opened her closet to loads of cute choices.

I quickly learned that having a friendly personality, cheerleading abilities, and a stylish appearance were the perfect recipe for popularity. Exactly what every seventh-grader wants.

Luckily, the first two ingredients came naturally for me. But I was lacking the clothes. The contents of my closet looked nothing like that of the country club girls and my fellow cheerleaders. Perhaps that turned out to be an advantage in the long term. What I lacked in wardrobe, I made up for in creativity. My desire to fit in made me think outside the box.

I borrowed an adorable outfit from my friend Lucy. I still remember how cute it was, a yellow peasant blouse with black polka dots and a little red bow with a matching flared skirt. It was very colorful, sweet, and each piece was easy to pair with other separates, which is what I did. First I wore the entire outfit together. Then I paired the top with my own sweater and another skirt or pants. A few days later, I paired the skirt with a different top of mine. Voila! By the time I gave it back to Lucy two weeks later, I'd made four different outfits. I didn't see it as vanity. I was simply doing what was called for to be successful in my world: making a silk purse out of... not a sow's ear, but definitely slim pickins.

Social convention at this school required me to make it *look like* I was wearing different things all the time, while what I was really doing was cleverly re-arranging sweaters, skirts, tops, and pants into various sets of getups and guises. Great training for the career I now hold!

My natural inclinations and resourcefulness served me well. I was beginning to develop a sense of style to express my creativity and uniqueness. I was able to pull off daring outfits and hairstyles because my confidence was growing and I felt happy being expressive.

In order to afford college, I took a job at downtown Chicago's Central National Bank. Reading the newspaper during a coffee break one morning, I noticed an advertisement announcing young women could win scholarship money for college. That ad turned out to be an entry form for a local beauty pageant, which would feed into the state pageant and eventually to the Miss America pageant.

In the Miss America system, prize money comes from business sponsorships
and is rewarded as tuition payment to an accredited college or university.
I'd never even considered being in a pageant before, and I realized I took a
somewhat dim view of that whole world. I anticipated the other contestants
being superficial, fake, and catty, wearing false eyelashes to bed. I suspected
they would each have their own hairdresser and makeup person and never eat
for fear of gaining an ounce. I worried I wouldn't fit in. I certainly wasn't the
stereotypical contestant; I was much more girl-next-door. Would they shun
me?

But for the most part, the girls were smart, talented, interesting young ladies. I
encountered no cattiness or displays of jealousy or meanness, the way you see
on a television murder mystery.

We received five straight days of coaching on poise, verbal communication
skills, body language, and etiquette. Some might consider this fluff, unnecessary, or non-essential to career advancement and professional development.
Little did I realize then that without cultivation of the three key points of
personal branding – appearance, body language, and communication – you
may miss millions of dollars of earning potential along with your personal
fulfillment. It was years later before I realized the value of that week's training.

I didn't realize how difficult it would be to stand in front of an audience of
three thousand people, walk with poise, and speak into a microphone with
assurance about my dreams and aspirations. But I won the local pageant and
went on to compete in the Miss Illinois pageant – an entire week of amazing
insights and personal growth.

I went away to college at Northern and then Western Illinois University. From
there I embarked on a career of acting and dancing in plays, musicals, film, and
commercials. I was blessed to work with some big names: Shelley Winters,
Robert Conrad, John Mahoney. I had amazing experiences.

I learned something from acting that applies to the work I do today. Actors
must change hairstyle, makeup, voice, wardrobe, posture, and energy to that of
their character.

From these experiences, I came to realize that people play many different roles in life. We dress differently for different situations depending on the occasion and who we'll be with. We all do that; it's simply what's called for.

In 2006, my youngest son was in his junior year in high school and my oldest was in college. They didn't need a full-time mom anymore and I wanted the fulfillment of a career. But what to do? I knew I wouldn't be happy punching a clock; that was too restrictive for me.

I couldn't think of a job I'd enjoy enough to stick with, except for acting in professional theater. But there wasn't enough commercial and film work in the Denver area, so although I still had an agent and landed occasional jobs in commercials and industrial films, acting in Colorado would never be a full-time career.

Around that time, my friend Robin asked me to help her shop for a profession-al wardrobe. In previous years, I'd helped my sister Vanessa and several friends put together outfits for parties and helped fellow dancers with costumes and performance makeup. I'd helped a neighbor choose a wardrobe for a trip to Europe. And I'd chosen every piece of my husband's clothing, shoes, and acces-sories, including his sports and exercise apparel, for many years.

All these things came so naturally to me that I never really thought about them. Well, Robin and I headed off to Nordstrom to find new presentation clothes for her. I picked out a knee-length, olive green, form-fitting skirt with a kick-pleat in the back and a tapered jacket to create a polished professional image.

She was in the dressing room when I heard, "Oh, I don't know if this is right for work, Marian. It seems awfully tight. Doesn't it make my butt look big?"

Robin was a size four.

"No, you look shapely," I said. "You're a beautiful woman; there's nothing wrong with that. The skirt fits you well, and it's absolutely appropriate for work. Put the jacket on and see how they look together." I coached her to button the buttons, rather than leave the jacket open. I handed her a pair of two-and-a-half inch black classic pumps to complete the look.

"These are kind of dressy for a scientist," she said, looking at the heels doubt-fully. She slipped them on.

"Oh wow!" Robin turned front to back and front again. "I never would have picked any of these, but I love everything! This whole thing is fantastic." She sucked in her cheeks and did a couple of pivots in front of the three-way mirror, like a model on a runway. A woman walking past commented, "That looks amazing." Robin took one more look in the mirror and bought the whole package.

On the way home, Robin expressed her excitement with her purchases and said, "You could do this."

"Do *what?*" I asked.

"Help people pick clothes they never would pick for themselves, but that look great on them," she answered.

"What *is* that?" I asked.

In her brilliance, Robin answered, "I don't know, but you should find out and make a business out of it."

So, in the spring of 2006, I stood in my kitchen thinking about what I could do for a career. I asked myself, "What do I love to do and how can I make a business out of it?" The answer was immediate. "I love to help people look as good as they can, so they feel confident and attractive – *better than they ever thought they could*. That's what I want to do."

I did a deep-dive into research. I joined the Association of Image Consultants International, the highest standard of credibility in the image industry. I studied for and passed their three-hour exam at Metro State College in Denver. I designed documents on how to dress to flatter your unique body type and developed a color system.

Clients started finding me online, and word of mouth spread. Organizations and groups asked me to speak to their members about business casual ward-robe, weekend style, and achieving an image that's sharp, smart, and profes-sional.

And the rest, as they say, is history.

I hope this book can help you to develop a style you absolutely love, one that expresses who you are and allows you to feel more confident in every situation. You get to choose whatever your heart and soul desire. You don't need a lot of money. You can experiment with colors, approach, tone and trend, depending on your personality, your level of playfulness, your feeling of power.

The wonderful thing about style is that it's fluid; you're not stuck in only one genre. You can try on and try out different designs, patterns, and trends. It's up to you.

My life's lessons have flavored my own approach to life, family, home, and work. They've taught and still teach me lessons relating to my path and my passion. They are the ingredients that drive my spirit and strength. I want every woman to feel the vitality, strength, and sparkle that awakens when you feel your most radiant, inside and out. I want you to know that it is absolutely possible to go through your day with pizzazz, zest, and zing. This book describes how to express your authentic self with polished presence and exquisite influence. I hope you will get out of it as much as I have put into it.

To your best style and best life,

Marian Rothschild

CHAPTER 1

YOUR TIME TO *Shine*

Congratulations! You've decided to make a change, for any number of reasons. Maybe you feel stuck in a style rut and don't know how to get out. Maybe you haven't had the exposure to fashion know-hows. Maybe your mom didn't have the knack to pass down beauty tips, or maybe style wasn't something that was stressed in your upbringing. Maybe you've just been very busy with life and other things took precedence.

Whatever the reason, it's understandable. I'm the first to admit in the grand scheme of things – universally speaking, cosmic consciousness-wise – wardrobe, hairstyles, and accessories are *not* the most important things. But in your daily life, dealing with people one-on-one, clients, customers, partners, prospective partners, and prospective clients, does appearance matter? You betcha! Your appearance sends an instant, nonverbal message about who you are to everyone who sees you – whether you like it or not.

Rather than rail against a youth-obsessed society, why not have some fun with it? You can dress to *express your inner essence* – who you are from the inside out. And that's not just fun, it's fulfilling. It might even be life-changing.

Taking the first step toward any type of change can be daunting. This book offers a gentle way to slide into a style update, in the comfort and convenience of your own home, at your own pace. It will be a fun, interesting, and empowering experience. You'll notice things you've never even considered before. You will start to look at your complete, head-to-toe appearance – clothing, accessories, and personal expression – with new possibilities in mind.

My hope is for this book to inspire you in many ways, because inspiration leads to transformation.

Be honest with yourself. The more honest you are, the more this book will help you discover and unveil your put-together, polished, personal style. Let's call it wardrobe therapy. Or fashion rehab. Or how about head-to-toe, inside-and-out image alteration? As with any type of therapy, it's solely for your benefit. It's a process, not a product.

Some of the questions in the Personal Style Assessment may be a struggle if you haven't thought about these issues before. No worries. Just give it some thought, and check in with your inner voice. Again, this is for you — your personal growth, insight, and self-knowledge. The insights you'll get can lead to understanding, empowerment, satisfaction — and some outstanding outfits that make you feel amazing to boot!

If, while filling in the personal style assessment portion of the book, something doesn't feel right, simply check in with your intuition. Ask yourself what your truth is. Deep inside you, it's there. If you get stuck, you can always go back to previous questions and add more information, update your status, expand your envelope.

This isn't about expectations or fitting in. It's not about following trends or keeping up with the Kardashians. Isn't that a relief? This personal style journey is about what's right for you, so you can express *yourself* from the inside out. It's about learning what flatters your shape, coloring, and features, what fits into your lifestyle, and feels like your *most beautiful and genuine self*. And that's different for each of us.

I believe women want to be vibrant, attractive, and genuine. I believe when you match your outer image to your personality, passions, and lifestyle you feel confident, authentic, and empowered. When you understand how to put together outfits that express the true you, how to dress to flatter your shape, what colors make your skin glow and your eyes sparkle — you can look and feel fantastic.

This book will address each of those issues. There are places on many of the pages for you to take notes, underline, and mark up, so you can apply solutions that fit your unique needs and lifestyle.

Enjoy the journey. Update and look great!

THE ART OF PERSONAL STYLE (It's never too late)

Everyone has a personal style. Right now, you may feel as if your style has been on the shelf for decades. Remember back to when you wore your hair, accessories, and clothes with flair and panache, or at least a certain special something that made your look uniquely your own? How long has it been?

If someone said to you, "That looks like something you'd wear," what would they mean? What would you *like* it to mean? The difference between what your wardrobe says about you now and what you'd like your signature look to be is what you'll be working on here.

Style is not fashion. That's an important point to remember. Fashion is what's trendy at the moment – what designers and department store CEOs are selling today. Anyone can buy the latest fashion; just ask any sales person what's hot right now and she'll happily sell it to you.

But it won't necessarily be right for you. It may not be the most flattering color choice for your unique coloring, or the most flattering line or shape on your figure. What's trendy right now may not fit your lifestyle or it may not go with anything else in your closet or it just may not feel like the real you.

Here's the biggest difference between fashion and style: fashion is extrinsic (from outside of yourself) and style is intrinsic. Style comes from your heart, your soul, your essential self. It also accumulates from your memories, your experiences, and your senses. But just like any message from deep within, your personal style can only be heard if you listen carefully.

Remember the last time you saw something like a painting or an amazing view that was so inspirational and beautiful that it touched you deeply, perhaps in an unexpected way? Those tiny yet meaningful experiences add a visceral memory to what is developing as your personal style.

Style is an attitude that affects your choices. It's selecting pieces and putting them together to express your unique character and unbridled spirit. It's also rejecting a whole lot of what designers and stores try to push, because that just *ain't your thang*. Style means deciding on wardrobe and accessories with conscious intention to represent your inner essence and your power as an individual. Style gives you intrigue and interest.

Choosing style over ho-hum is an expression of self-respect and honor. Taking the time to clean, press, and put together a lovely outfit shows you care about yourself and whomever you will be with, to make that effort. It's the opposite of trying to impress. Impressing is shallow and superficial; honoring is deep and soulful. When you dress with thoughtful intention, you'll feel the purpose and the power behind it.

Doing your hair and makeup, adding a scarf, earrings, and cute pumps may seem like it's a lot of trouble, but think about the rewards. It's like the feelings you get after eating lots of healthy food and going to the gym four days in a row. You feel *so* good! You're taking care of yourself. You feel empowered, right? And confident. And attractive. *Nothin' wrong with that!*

Style is an equal-opportunity purveyor. Every woman, whether princess, professor, or punk rocker can stylize herself as a unique individual. You don't need a lot of money; what you need is information. As you learn, experience, and grow, your personal style will evolve. Especially when you nourish it, encourage it, and enhance it. How?

Be sincere.

Be sensitive.

And be selective.

LOOK GOOD — WHEN?

Every week I meet women who tell me they know they need to update their wardrobe, but they're waiting. They're waiting to lose weight, get a raise, change jobs, sell the house, catch a mouse, eat a fish. The list goes on.

Can you relate? Are you one of those people who know that you need to make a change, but you are also looking for any excuse under the sun *not* to change? I admit change can be hard. But change can also be exhilarating, expansive, liberating, and empowering.

Change seems difficult before you get started because you don't know what to expect. Moving across the country to a new state, starting a job you've never done before in a place where you know no one – *that's* hard. Raising kids on your own, climbing out of debt, battling illness – *that's* hard. You may have done something that was very, very difficult. You lived through it. And you learned a lot, I'll bet. We've all fought battles that pushed us to our very edge, forced us to pull superhuman strength from our deepest core.

But cleaning out your closet? That's not hard. Not in the universal scheme of things. Neither is looking at magazines and deciding what you like and don't. And shopping? By the time you've worked through my Personal Style Assessment and all of the subsequent chapters, shopping will be much easier and more satisfying for you than you've ever dreamed it could be.

Bottom line – if you sit around and wait for the perfect set of circumstances and the perfect time to upgrade your style, nothing will change.

The perfect time is now. The perfect place is wherever you are.

Seize the moment, grab a pen, and get ready to say hello to the new, chic-er, sleeker, updated you.

CHAPTER 2

PERSONAL *Style* ASSESSMENT

Here we go!

Describe your current wardrobe. *(Circle all that apply.)*

Mostly black and grey   Colorful

Boring   Outdated

Eclectic   Flashy

Too casual   Trendy

Wrong size   Mismatched

What else?

_____

_____

_____

Which parts of your wardrobe are working for you?
What's not working?

Working:

_____

_____

_____

Not Working:

_____

_____

_____

Briefly describe your lifestyle right now.

_____

_____

What are your activities? What you do weekdays and evenings, and on the weekends during the day and in the evenings?

_____

_____

What are your professional goals, and how soon could they happen?

_____

_____

List any and all personal goals you'd like to work toward.

_____

_____

Based on your personal and professional goals, list some additional activities you'd like to work into your lifestyle in the next few months.

_____

_____

What percentage of each of these categories must your wardrobe be dedicated to? _(Some categories may overlap.)_

_____ Business attire

_____ Nice casual (weekend parties, going out with friends, dates)

_____ Attractive athletic wear

_____ Formal/semi-formal (sequins, sparkles)

_____ Comfy cozy at-home only

List the areas of your life where you'd like to look good.

_____

_____

_____

What would you like your appearance to say about you? Circle those words that really resonate with your true inner self.

Smart	Healthy	Sophisticated
Put-together	Competent	Comfortable
Professional	Confident	Artistic
Approachable	Friendly	Powerful
Attractive	Genuine	Interesting
Creative	Cool	Available
Unique	Classy	Authoritative
Sensual	Sexy	Respectable
Practical	Dignified	Innovative
Original	Ladylike	Vibrant
Adorable	Sassy	Exotic
Warm	Poised	Spiritual

What else?

_____

_____

_____

The words you selected are your **STYLE WORDS**. Let these adjectives be your guideline to great style, the keys to dressing to express your inner essence. For every situation, before choosing an outfit, ask yourself who you're going to be with and **what message would you'd like to send about who you are.**

Who are your style inspirations? Celebrities, news personalities, actors, musicians, friends, co-workers, etc.? List as many as possible.

_____

_____

What do you love to wear?

_____

_____

What would you never wear?

_____

_____

When getting dressed for work and other occasions, what challenges do you experience? *(Check which ones apply to you.)*

- [ ] Don't have time
- [ ] Nothing fits right
- [ ] Can't afford the quality I'd like
- [ ] Don't know what goes with what
- [ ] Don't know what looks good on me
- [ ] Not sure what to wear for the occasion
- [ ] Closet too packed with the wrong stuff

What else? _____

_____

_____

Do you feel stuck in a certain type of clothing?

☐ Yes ☐ No

If so, describe this style.

Frumpy	Just not me	All black
Not flattering	Way too casual	Outdated
Boring	Not age-appropriate	Too big/too small
No pizzazz		

What else?

_____

_____

_____

What are your goals for your personal image? Why are you doing this work now? What do you want to change?

_____

_____

Dig deep for this one. It's not as superficial as some of the other questions. **What gets in the way of your essence and personal style shining through?**

☐ My weight   ☐ I don't have the knack for it

☐ My budget   ☐ I don't have the knowledge

☐ My closet is a mess   ☐ Not sure what looks good on me

☐ Time management   ☐ My past experiences

What else?

_____

_____

Check which styles of clothing you'd like more of, for professional and weekend wear.

Relaxed

Trendy

Chic

Sexy

Dramatic

Creative

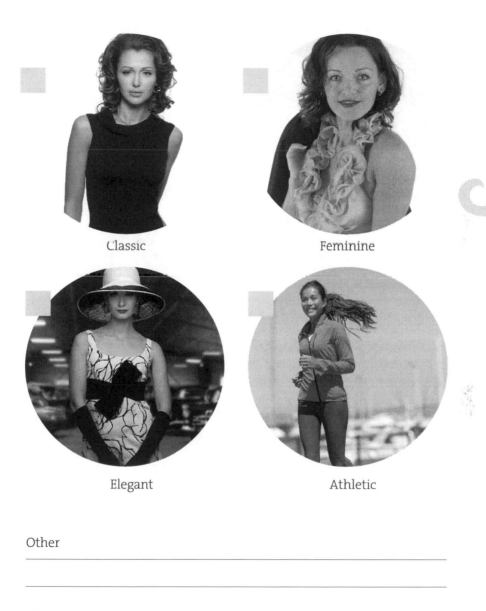

Classic

Feminine

Elegant

Athletic

Other

_____

_____

_____

_____

_____

What are your challenges when shopping?

- Department stores are overwhelming
- Don't know what looks good on me
- Not sure what department to shop in
- Don't trust the sales people
- Not sure what store to shop in
- Don't have the time to shop
- Don't have the budget
- Don't enjoy shopping

Do you feel that your makeup needs updating?

- Yes
- No

If you answered yes, I recommend you have a makeup lesson from a makeup artist – not at a department store counter, if you can help it. The salespeople in the cosmetics department of a store are *usually* not trained makeup consultants. They may have been selling carpets or cat toys the month before. Also, it's their job to sell. They get paid for selling product, not for teaching technique and color theory. They may think they know these things, and I'm sure they love applying makeup.

However, in my experience, some cosmetics sales people can't tell whether you need foundation with a rosy tint or a yellow tint. The fluorescent lighting in department stores can be atrocious for matching colors. Clients show me foundations, concealers, and lip colors sold to them in shades and formulas completely wrong for their skin.

When you're trying to improve your image, bad makeup is the last thing you need. I don't recommend trusting your beautiful face to anyone other than a trained professional. Ask your hairstylist, esthetician, or other beauty professional for a recommendation of a good makeup artist. Some day spas and hair salons also have makeup artists who give lessons. Ask reliable professionals in your area.

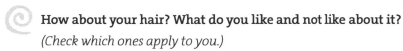

How about your hair? What do you like and not like about it?

(Check which ones apply to you.)

- Outdated style
- Love my hair and everything about it
- Not sure if the color is good for me
- Not sure if the style is right for me
- Don't know what style would be better
- Don't know where to go for the truth
- Not sure what products to use

What else?

_____

_____

Truth be known, in parts of my life, I'd really like to become more...

(Circle which words apply to you.)

Bold	Flexible	Healthy
Mature	Relaxed	Focused
Organized	Courageous	Trusting
Positive	Peaceful	Outgoing
Intellectual	Refined	Feminine
Open-minded	Athletic	Dignified
Sensitive	Approachable	Authoritative
Fun	Fancy	Unique
Active	Ambitious	Slim
Powerful	Educated	Respected

Other

_____

_____

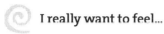 **I really want to feel...**

Cute	Pretty	Sensual
Sexy	Athletic	Glamorous
Youthful	Mature	Sensible
Playful	Adventurous	Professional
Confident	Empowered	Fulfilled

Other

_____

_____

Every adjective that you selected above are also more of your **STYLE WORDS**. Remember them, embody them, and use them often to inspire you to **put together looks that express those ideas.**

 **Rank your most urgent needs.**
(Rank from 1 – 10, 1 being highest priority, 10 being lowest priority.)

_____ Finding the best hairstyle for me

_____ Learning to avoid shopping mistakes

_____ Learning how to do wardrobe editing and organization

_____ Learning which colors are most flattering on me

_____ Understanding what to wear for different situations

_____ Knowing what wardrobe necessities I should have

_____ Figuring out if certain separates look good together

_____ Creating a variety of outfits with separates and accessories

_____ Understanding which styles and shapes are most flattering

_____ Updating my makeup techniques to be more realistic for my lifestyle

Now that you've done some soul-searching and inner reflection, circle whichever personality styles best fit you.
(There may be several, that's okay)

Relaxed	Trendy	Chic
Sexy	Dramatic	Creative
Classic	Feminine	Elegant

Other

_____

_____

Great job! You might never have thought about these things previously, so some of them may have caught you off guard. If you couldn't fill in the blanks right away, that's fine. Give it some thought. Go back to the unanswered questions in a day or two. Something surprising might occur to you between now and then. Keep filling in answers as new ideas pop up. There will be lots more deep diving ahead.

It's an inner journey first and foremost. Questions lead to growth and understanding, which leads to actualization and change. You must know yourself in order to make any kind of transformation. You're on your way.

Every person on this planet is utterly individual. No two people, even identical twins, have the exact same coloring, features, shape, clothing taste, preferences, and lifestyle. The more you know about yourself, the more you can help yourself look and feel your best. You deserve to look and feel genuinely gorgeous, truly terrific, and smartly sensational. Don't settle for anything less!

Now that you've answered those very personal questions, you're ready to learn how to best flatter your unique body, head-to-toe.

CHAPTER 3

SECRETS OF *Shape*, LINE AND BODY TYPE

To realistically assess your overall shape, you'll need to take a deep breath and agree to be completely honest. This is so hard for us women, isn't it? We're either too critical of flaws no one else even sees or in complete denial of things we refuse to see. But no one else is watching or reading this; it's only for you. When you have accurate information, you can dress to *flatter your shape*, not hide it or inadvertently emphasize those parts you don't like.

The main idea of dressing to flatter your shape is to *accentuate your attributes and camouflage your non-favorables*. It's that simple! But the simplicity of that idea doesn't mean that it's easy. We're attached to our bodies, so we take every little flaw personally. Be gentle on yourself. No one is perfect. No one.

We all have things we feel insecure about. If you ask any beautiful woman what she doesn't like about her body, she'd have plenty to say, believe me. I've posed the questions in this book to hundreds of women. These questions are also part of my in-person Color, Style, and Wardrobe Consultation. Some of the women I work with are knockouts. You'd never guess they could find anything unfavorable about their looks. And yet we all have things we wish were different. Have you ever met a curly-haired woman who didn't wish her hair was straight? And vice versa?

We can change some things about our bodies. Like weight, for instance. Most of the women I've worked with would love to weigh between five and thirty-five pounds less. Losing weight is difficult but not impossible. You have to want it bad enough to make some major changes in eating and exercise habits.

Other things about our bodies can't be changed. We can't change our height, underlying skin tone, shape of our legs (except to firm them up with more exercise), size of our shoulders, or length of our necks. But there is beauty in our uniqueness.

And, here's the really great news — we can change our *appearance* by high-lighting our attributes. We can use the basic design principles of color, shape, line, texture, contrast, and focus to vary and alter the appearance of our physi-cal bodies, head to toe.

It's a fascinating journey. And it can be fun. Just like so many pursuits in life, you'll get out of this what you put into it. It's worth the effort. Be bold.

YOUR SHAPE

To correctly assess your shape, look in a full-length mirror while naked or in your undies. Yes, you heard me! Position yourself or the mirror so you can only see your body, not your head. The mirror should visually cut you off at the neck. This is to get some distance, so the body reflected back at you seems like just any random body, not necessarily your own. This will help you detach emotionally and therefore be more honest.

Got the mirror set up so you can only see your body, not your face?

Good. Now use your hands to frame the shape in the mirror. Adjust your hands to fit around the reflection of the body's shape. What shape have your hands created? In other words, objectively speaking, what overall shape is your body, realistically?

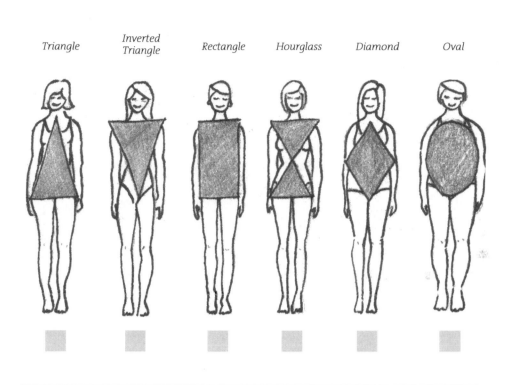

Triangle   Inverted Triangle   Rectangle   Hourglass   Diamond   Oval

Women come in all different shapes and sizes. Always have, always will. Just ask the 17th century baroque painter, Rubens. No one size or shape is better than others, although you might have a preference. The ideal for any woman is to be healthy, happy, and balanced in mind, body, and spirit. I can't change your body's overall form, but there are definitely ways to use color, shape, line, and focus to alter the way you *appear,* and that's where the magic starts. Here are some shape-shifting strategies to flatter your unique shape:

TRIANGLE

Triangles are larger on the bottom half and smaller up top. In other words, your hips are at least a bit wider than your shoulders and/or bust. Balance your figure with clothes that taper in at the waist and give the appearance of narrowing at the hips and widening at the shoulders.

DO:

- Wear light or bright colors and patterns on top, dark colors on the bottom.

- Wear tops with strong shoulder seams that match up with your shoulder. Skip the raglans and halter tops, sorry!

- Wear tops with large collars, preferably with lapels that point outward.

- Find blouses, shirts, sweaters, and jackets with horizontal stripes, capped sleeves, soft shoulder pads, and other accents at the shoulder area.

- Wear flattering colors next to your face. This includes all tops, necklaces, earrings, and scarves.

- Wear large cowl-neck collars and wide necklines, like boat-neck or square necked sweaters and T-shirts. Toss those drab crew necks.

- Wear scarves tied around your shoulders so they give a wide horizontal look rather than hanging down your body in a vertical line. Think pashmina wraps, not neckties.

- Wear jackets, tunics, and long sweaters that cover your rear.

- Pop the collar of crisp blouses. Depending on the situation, perhaps open a button or two.

DO NOT:

- Wear light or white pants, shorts, or skirts.

- Wear collarless tops or jackets.

- Buy sweaters or jackets with a peplum (flares outward) or any other accent at the hip line.

- Wear cropped jackets and tops that end at the waist.

- Choose pants, skirts, or shorts with side pockets that stick out, or with embellished back pockets that call attention to the caboose.

DO:

- Choose pants and skirts in light or bright colors.

- Keep patterns, accents, and embellishments on the lower half of the body.

- Wear boot-cut or flare-leg pants to balance out the upper half of your body.

- Choose capri pants and ballet flats to show skin down below.

- Choose A-line, tulip, or flared skirts and dresses, especially if they have a pattern or focal point like an embroidered design below the waist.

- Show off shapely gams with knee-length skirts, dresses, and Bermuda shorts. If you've got 'em, flaunt 'em!

- Wear bare legs, ultra sheer hose, nude hose, or colored tights and heels whenever possible.

- Choose collarless tops, raglan sleeves, and halter tops.

- Wear dark colors on top, light or bright colors on the bottom.

- Wear scarves that hang down in a long vertical line and end in a diagonal hem, not straight across horizontal.

- Find jackets and sweaters with a peplum at the waist or that flare out at the hem, so that your hips will look larger and balance out your figure.

- Roll or push up your sleeves on blouses, shirts, sweaters, and jackets to the elbow area to show some forearm. Bracelet length sleeves will look great, too.

DO NOT:

- Wear puffy sleeves or thick shoulder pads; they will only make your shoulders look larger.

- Wear anything to make your upper half look larger, like big, thick wool scarves bundled around your neck.

- Be fooled into thinking that horizontal stripes up top are good. Stick to vertical stripes up top and wear horizontal stripes and other prints on your bottom half.

INVERTED TRIANGLE

Inverted triangles have wide shoulders and/or large busts, tapering to narrow hips. Balance by visually diminishing the size of your upper body and widening your hips. Instant va-va-va-voom!

RECTANGULAR

Straight up and down athletic figures without much definition at the waist fall into the rectangle category. You can work some balancing magic to create an hourglass shape. Here are some tricks:

DO:

• Choose dresses, jackets, and tops that taper at the waist to make you look curvier.

• Try to visually widen the shoulders and hips by wearing V-necks, wide collars, and gathered sleeves.

• Wear pencil skirts and pants with wide back pockets.

• Pull in your waistline with a belt, sash, darts, or side panels in a dark color.

• Look for tapered waistlines on everything you wear; all tops, dresses, and even coats.

• Find jackets and cardigans with a fitted shape, hopefully even a peplum flaring out from the waist.

• Try high-waisted pants that will add curves to your shape. Curves are good!

• Accessorize with scarves and jewelry that you love.

DO NOT:

• Wear boxy tops like men's T-shirts or square, cropped jackets. If a piece of clothing is shaped like a box, it will make you look like a box. (Remember, curves are good!)

• Let rolls show through thin fabric; wear a sturdy camisole under tops. (See section on body slimmers in Chapter Nine.)

• Feel that there's no hope. If you look more feminine, you will feel more feminine.

DO:

- Wear wrap dresses and tops that crisscross at the bust or waistline. Classic yet sexy, what could be better?

- Wear tops with collars and V-necklines.

- Show off your tapered waist with belts, sashes, and knee-length dresses and skirts.

- Try jackets and sweaters that flare out just below the waist.

- Wear boot-leg or flare-leg pants which repeat the hourglass shape, reiterating femininity in the mind's eye.

- Use a body shaper to hold in a tummy, just below the belly button. Body shapers are a girl's best friend, never mind the diamonds.

- Accentuate your great shape with scarves, jewelry, and heels.

DO NOT:

- Wear clingy/too tight tops and miniskirts, especially if not age-appropriate. Use discretion!

- Think that boxy and shapeless clothes are fine.

HOURGLASS

If you've got this classic shape, you're lucky; an hourglass figure can look sexy, striking, and lovely. You won't need too many tricks to alter your shape, unless it's your size that's an issue.

DIAMOND

A diamond body shape has narrow shoulders and average sized hips, with most of the weight distributed through the midriff and waist area. These tips will help you do a balancing act.

DO:

- Wear tops, long scarves, and necklaces in colors that flatter your skin tone or match your eye color.

- Try a V-neckline to draw the eye inward, and light or bright colors underneath a darker jacket or sweater to put the focus right where you want it: on your beautiful face.

- Try to occasionally dress monochromatically (all one color), or mono-tonal (lighter and darker shades of the same tone).

- Wear tops and sweaters that drape loosely, are tunic-length, and have structured shoulders. Trés chic!

- Wear fabrics that skim the body. No clinging or drooping.

- Use a sturdy body slimmer to pull in the tummy and midriff section. There are great brands to choose from in lingerie departments or specialty stores.

- Wear light, bright, and shiny colors up by your face with necklaces, earrings, scarves, and lip color.

DO NOT:

- Wear anything overly fitted or tailored through the waist.

- Wear all black, all the time. That gets dreary and fools no one. There are so many lovely colors that will make your skin glow and your eyes sparkle!

- Let rolls show through thin fabric; wear a sturdy camisole under tops. (See the section on body slimmers in Chapter Nine. They just might change your life.)

- Neglect your posture; always walk, stand, and sit up straight.

DO:

- Wear lighter or brighter colors under a dark jacket or sweater, for that attractive pop of color.

- Wear vertical lines: seams, zippers, stripes, lightweight scarves, and long necklaces in flattering colors down the center of your body.

- Wear tops and sweaters that drape, are tunic-length, and have structured shoulders.

- Wear V-necklines that draw the eye inward and put the focus on your beautiful face. (But not so low that they pull the focus onto "the girls.")

- Try a sturdy body slimmer to pull in the tummy and midriff section. There are great brands to choose from in lingerie departments or specialty stores.

- Wear light, bright, and shiny colors by your face, using necklaces, earrings, scarves, and lip color.

DO NOT:

- Wear anything overly fitted or tailored through the waist.

- Wear clothes that are too tight or too baggy; they will not do you any favors. You need the perfect fit, even if a tailor has to be called in occasionally to do the job.

- Wear very long necklaces or other accessories that put the focal point at the waist.

- Wear all black, all the time. It fools no one and there are so many lovely colors that will make your skin glow and your eyes sparkle!

- Neglect your posture; always walk, stand, and sit up straight.

OVAL

A classic oval is broader through the middle and upper torso, with no waist indentation and often with a full bust and sloping shoulders. You'll be surprised to find out how much you can do to minimize your stomach area and elongate your overall body length.

PETITE

Petite is an ever-so-sweet way of saying "short." Basically, you are classified as petite if you are 5'2" and under. Doesn't matter if you wear a size 2 or 12, if you find that you need a step stool to look in your front door peephole, you are considered petite.

DO:

• Shop in the Petite section of your favorite department or women's clothing store to find clothes that properly fit your proportions.

• Add the appearance of length to your torso with scarves tied in low-hanging knots, and the remainder of the scarf hanging vertical, down the center of your body.

• Adorn yourself with long necklaces in single, double, or triple strands down the center of your torso.

• Look for clothes with vertical seams, zippers, ruffles, buttons, and diagonal pockets to add the appearance of length.

• Wear jackets and sweaters long and lean, but not so long as to overpower you.

• Purchase tunic-length tops that hit right below the hips and taper in at the waist.

• Wear pants slim and straight, but not too tight.

• Wear skirts and dresses right around knee length, give or take an inch or two.

• Find Bermuda length, (just above the knee) shorts for summer time.

• Flatter yourself with bracelet-length sleeves.

• Push sweater sleeves up to just below the elbow.

• Wear heals, preferably 2" or higher, on shoes, sandals, and knee-high boots.

• Hem pants to ¾" from the floor, no matter what shoes you are wearing.

• Look for platform shoes and boots to add extra height without discomfort.

• Lengthen your look with low V-necks and elongated collars.

- Pick classic pumps and other shoes that show as much of your foot as possible. This will give the illusion of elongating your legs.

- Ask friends for a referral to a terrific tailor who can tweak what you already have for a more vertical look.

- Go bare-legged in warm weather. This will also elongate the appearance of your legs.

- Dress monochromatically or mono-tonally; same color or tone all over. Match shoes and stockings to skirts, pants, tops, and dresses.

- Wear socks the same color as your pants and shoes.

- Ask your hairdresser for a hairstyle with vertical shapes instead of horizontal lines.

DO NOT:

- Wear cuffs on pants.

- Think that boxy jackets or sweaters look sweet. (They look like a box.)

- Let your slacks or jeans be shorter than ¾" from the floor, unless they are the Audrey Hepburn style of ankle-length slacks.

- Buy shoes or sandals with ankle straps.

- Overwhelm your appearance with chunky jewelry, large prints, and clunky shoes and boots.

- Cut off your foot visually by wearing shoes and sandals with big, dark straps across the top of your foot. (That's valuable real estate!)

- Get sucked into wearing trends that include horizontal stripes anywhere on your body.

- Cut bangs straight across your forehead. (They should be long and swept off to the side.)

- Speak in a small, squeaky voice. You are an intelligent, insightful, amazing woman; communicate accordingly.

TALL AND THIN

Tall and thin is what many of us aspire to. However, some women find their height a detriment. This may be especially true if you are extremely thin as well. Appreciate your gifts. You know that saying, "The grass is always greener..."

DO:

- Create horizontal lines across the body whenever and wherever possible; pockets, stripes, piping, zippers, and panels on tops, jackets, skirts and dresses.

- Don short necklaces and lots of bracelets.

- Color blocking will work great for you with contrasting colored tops, bottoms, and belts.

- Drape scarves in a horizontal line across your shoulders, or in an infinity knot. (Watch a Youtube video on tying scarves.)

- Go ahead and wear ankle straps on shoes or sandals.

- Look for cuffs on slacks and trousers.

- Wear Capri's or ankle length pants and jeans, but not too tight.

- Stand up straight - just wear flats or a low heal.

- Ask your hairstylist for a short, blunt cut, no longer than shoulder length.

- Add volume with pants and jeans that are boot cut or flared-leg.

- Push up sweater sleeves to just below the elbow .

- Break up height with horizontal lines by wearing belts in a variety of colors, even on top of sweaters and dresses.

DO NOT:

- Slouch or stand with bad posture.

- Hang scarves and necklaces long and down the center of your body.

- Apologize for your height.

- Wear vertical stripes or super skinny jeans.

- Give up by wearing masculine-looking clothes or avoiding your femininity.

From the top of your head to the tip of your toes, what are your favorite parts?

Eyes	Bust	Lips/smile
Hair	Waist	Hands/wrists
Midsection	Rear end	Legs
Feet	Skin	Arms

What else?

_____

_____

_____

_____

What are your least favorite parts?

Eyes	Bust	Lips/smile
Hair	Waist	Hands/wrists
Midsection	Rear end	Legs
Feet	Skin	Arms

What else?

_____

_____

_____

_____

MARIAN'S RULES FOR DRESSING TO FLATTER YOUR BODY TYPE

1. **Accentuate your attributes and camouflage your non-desirables!**

   When creating outfits, put the focal point — where the eye goes first — on your favorite body parts. (I don't want to hear that you have no favorite body parts. Get over that.) Create the focal point by rocking bright colors and/or prints in the chosen area. Or place a beautiful pin or other bright embellishment near your most flattering features. It's so worth the effort to scour boutiques and jewelry departments for terrific necklaces and earrings. You want people to look at your face and the immediate area surrounding it.

   As far as the areas of your body that are your least favorite, simply cover them up or downplay them. Wear dark colors or cover up with tunic-length cardigans, sweaters or jackets, pretty scarves, long pants or boots.

   If you have great legs, flaunt them by wearing skirts and dresses. If you don't have the best knees but do have shapely calves, wear skirts that hit right at the middle or bottom of the knee. Very chic. (A great, cost effective option: take your skirts and dresses to a tailor and have them hemmed to the middle of your knees.)

   If you really don't like your knees, wear capris instead of shorts in warm weather. Make sure they hit you mid-calf and do not have cargo pockets on the side of the knee.

   If you have a lovely waistline but that un-flatten-able pooch bulges out right beneath it, wear a two-and-a-half-inch belt *just below the waist* to pull in and flatten out that irrepressible tummy. Sneaky but brilliant! Buy empire-waist tops that gather just under the bust and fall gently over the belly area, but taper on the sides. Also consider investing in a body slimmer. (See Chapter Nine.)

   In summary, whichever area you place accents, accessories, and bright colors will stand out. Wherever you put darker, solid colors will recede. What you cover up won't show. Know your strong points, and dress accordingly.

2. Fabrics

The choice of fabric can make an astonishing difference. Clothing should skim the body, never cling or droop. If you have sloping shoulders or a triangle shape, wear jackets made of sturdy fabric and tops made of crisp fabric to define the shoulders. Beware of inexpensive garments made of flimsy, limp fabric — every lump and bump on your back, belly, and behind will be magnified. Also, cheap fabrics don't hold up well to machine washers and dryers and will most likely wrinkle up, shrink up, twist up, or ball up after only a few washings. So *up* with better quality fabrics! (And always read washing instructions!)

3. Prints

When assembling outfits, try to use at least one item with some sort of print: checks, plaid, florals, geometric shapes, stripes, animals, or my favorite, polka dots. Everyone needs some gorgeous, appealing prints in their wardrobe. Usually we like to wear prints in a blouse or scarf. That's a plus; it puts the focal point right up by the face, where we want people to look.

The size of the print you wear depends on what size of a person you are. If you are petite, wear small prints. If you are a medium-sized woman, wear medium-sized prints, and if you're a big beauty, well, you've got it by now. Patterns that are too tiny for your frame won't balance your proportions, and prints that are too large for your frame will overwhelm your appearance.

Perhaps you've seen all those mixed prints in fashion magazines? You can **wear two prints together** – *if and only if* there is at least one shared color in both prints, and if one print is bolder and the other is more subtle. (Think of a man's tweed suit coat, pin-striped dress shirt, and wide-striped tie.)

Do wear vertical stripes for a slimming effect. Do not wear horizontal stripes unless you have a triangle shape, or a body mass index less than twenty. (That means you're pretty darn slim.) I know that horizontal stripes are all the rage right now, but you have to make an executive decision whether you're going to dress for fashion or to flatter your body type. It's up to you. Once you know the rules, you can decide which ones to break. After all, you are the boss of your appearance!

4. **Fit**

    Shoulder seams should line up with your shoulders, not ride too close to your neck, stick out beyond your shoulders, or hang down below your natural shoulder line. Long-sleeves should hit your hand, just below the wrist. Blouses, tops, and dresses should skim the body, not cling. You don't want gaps or bulges showing between shirt buttons, which will happen if the fabric is pulled too tight. And no, trying to close that gap with a safety pin is never classy! If the blouse fits very well other than buttons bulging, use Hollywood Fashion Tape (available at fabric stores) to close the gap.

    When trying on jackets and coats, be sure to move your arms around. Simulate driving a car, reaching up for something on a high shelf, etc. When trying on slacks, shorts, and skirts, be sure to sit down and see how tight the slacks are and how high the skirt or shorts ride up on your legs. Also watch for pants that pull too far down in the back when you sit, exposing your undies or worse.

5. **Comfort**

    Comfort is king – or should I say queen? But don't confuse comfort with slouchy, boring, or frumpy. Cute, flattering clothes can absolutely be comfortable. Nothing should pinch (too tight) or sag (too loose). I love the look of stretch jeans, but I can't wear them. On my legs, the fabric pulls too tight. Let's just say I'm not comfortable in them for more than a minute and a half. They look good but feel bad.

    However, you can find truckloads of trendy, chic, classic, and other sensational styles that are still comfortable. There are even a gazillion pairs of comfortable, cute shoes out there waiting for you to find them. (See my list of brand names in Chapter Eight.) Yes, it takes time and effort, but it will be worth it!

REAL-LIFE WOMEN

Kim is of average height with a triangle shape. Her shoulders are quite narrow compared to her hips. Kim slips easily into size 4 or 6 slacks, so you can imagine how tiny her upper body is. Our challenge was to accentuate her upper body and show off her small waist, while visually decreasing the size of her hips.

I suggested she wear only light or bright colors on top and darker colors on bottom. Kim had lots of colorful T-shirts in her wardrobe. We paired them with bright necklaces and wrapped patterned scarves around her neck and shoulders in creative ways, to add width where she needed it.

(Check YouTube for videos showing fun and interesting ways to tie scarves. Bet you'll be astounded.)

On our shopping trip, we found lots of tops with horizontal stripes, wide collars, cap sleeves, soft shoulder pads, and other embellishments up near the shoulder area. All of these accents helped make her shoulders appear wider. This balanced out her hips and gave her that much sought-after appearance of an hourglass figure. She loved the look!

When Kim tried on some of the skirts and dresses, I noticed her gorgeous, shapely legs. She'd been hiding these treasures! I encouraged her to wear cute skirts and shorts in dark colors that hit just above the knee.

If like many of us, you always have a gap between the waist of your jeans and your back, get yourself The Hip Hugger, a product with a clip on each end and elastic in the middle. Clip each end to your side belt loops, with the elastic part under your back belt loop. It holds your jeans in without having to wear a belt, so there's no big bulge up front, nor in back. The Hip Hugger is available at fabric stores in the notions department.

We found several great dresses for her to wear to friends' weddings. One had capped sleeves and color-blocking that was perfect for her figure type, with light hues on the upper half and darker shades below the waist.

The other dress also had capped sleeves. The top of the dress was a boxy shift with horizontal stripes, and the bottom fit snugly around her hips without being too tight. Because the shape of the dress was more horizontal and loose on top and more fitted on the bottom, it made her upper body appear larger. Her hips and thighs looked smaller in comparison. It was exactly the effect we wanted – a feminine yet balanced shape.

We had the tailor hem these dresses to just above Kim's knees, to showcase her shapely legs. Bare legs and classic pumps in nude give the appearance of another highly sought-after attribute – legs that go on for days! (Nude colored pumps will elongate your legs because they are the same color as your skin, yet give your foot a sexy, curvy line that's gorgeous!) A chic necklace of trendy large pearls finished off this simple yet elegant look. Best of all, Kim said she'd never felt so beautiful. Although she felt somewhat overwhelmed at the change, she was glowing.

CHAPTER 4

COLOR, CONTRAST, *and You*, OH MY!

Most women have always wondered which colors make your skin glow and your eyes sparkle; which are the right colors for your complexion and skin tone. No one wants to wander around looking washed out, slightly off kilter, ten years older than they are. This is what the wrong colors can do for you. The right colors make you radiant!

Sometimes you're drawn to certain reds or greens, but you're not exactly sure why, or if they are the best choices for you. Friends may say a certain color looks pretty on you, but you wonder if they're just being... well... friendly. Let's take the guesswork out of choosing those perfect, face-flattering hues. The first step is to know your skin tone. I'm talking warm vs. cool, the foundation of color theory.

My mother's Irish ancestry gave her fair skin that burns easily. My father's Central European ancestry gave him quick-tanning skin with a yellowish-beige hue. My four siblings and I inherited my dad's warm skin tone.

No type of skin tone is better or worse than another. It's just helpful to know what type you have, so you can pick colors that flatter it. Take a look at your un-tanned legs or places the sun has never seen. Does your un-tanned skin have a:

- Rosy color/bluish tone (cool)

- Yellow/golden tone (warm)

If you're not sure of your skin tone, compare your untanned legs to a friend's, your child's, or your partner's.

If you're still not sure, answer the following questions:

1. When you were a teenager lying in the midday sun for thirty minutes, would you:
   A. Burn or not get much color.
   B. Get a nice little tan or burn ever so slightly, then turn tan the next day.

2. After working out vigorously for an hour, is your face:
   A. Really red and it stays red for a while.
   B. Maybe a little red, but it doesn't stay red for very long.

3. Do you tan?
   A. Hardly ever. Maybe by the very end of summer there's a bit of tan, but mostly you burn, therefore you stay out of the sun.
   B. Pretty easily, even when just gardening or walking the dog.

If your answers were all choice A, you most likely have rosy or cool coloring. If your answers were all choice B, you surely have yellow or warm undertones to your skin.

It is possible to have a combination, or a neutral skin tone, but this is quite rare. Usually, we tend toward either warm or cool undertones. Whichever it is, the same principles of finding flattering colors will apply to all skin types.

Circle which is you, generally.

Rosy, with cool undertones

Yellow, with warm undertones

Generally speaking, those of you with rosy undertones to your skin look best in cool reds; maroon, wine, burgundy, pinkish coral, and fuchsia. Rosy undertones usually do not look good in orange or yellow; they are just not flattering to pink skin.

On the other hand, if you have yellow undertones or very golden skin, you do look good in orange, rust, and yellow, especially gold and honey colors. Your reds will be more of an orange-red; brick, russet, dark coral, and copper tones.

Everyone looks terrific in some shades of coral and aqua. That's because coral is halfway between pink and orange, and aqua is halfway between blue and green. I think all women should have several different tops, scarves, and necklaces in shades of peach and coral. Those colors look great up against your face because you have some shades of coral and peach tones in your face. However, as you'll see in the next section, your hair plays a major role in deciding what colors are best for you. So don't toss anything just yet.

Hair color is a huge factor when figuring out what category of coloring you fall into. We like to change it up a bit when it comes to hair color, ladies, don't we? Hey, I do it, too. But we're talking about you here, and you need to figure out exactly what colors your hair is *when you really love it*. When it feels like the real you.

So if your hair isn't currently your favorite color, if it's all darker roots and faded ends, make an appointment or go buy that bottle of color you loved so much when you used it before.

Ready? OK, take a mirror next to a window. You need to be facing both the mirror and the window. Take a good, hard gander at the colors in your hair right now. There may be four or five different shades or tones in your hair, even if you don't color it. For example, light brown, chestnut brown, medium brown, golden blond, copper, etc. Be as specific as possible, and write all the different colors that you see:

_____

_____

_____

If the colors in your hair are copper, golden, strawberry blond, or light, medium, and/or dark brown with some gold or honey colors, you most likely have warm tones in your hair color.

If you hair is more mousy grey, brown turning to grey, silver, ash blond, or black, your hair color has cool tones.

When you're sure which category you are, circle your coloring.

Hair: Warm or Cool   Skin: Warm or Cool

How light or dark is your hair? It matters. White hair is the lightest, all the way through the browns (medium), to black. How light or dark is your hair? *Circle your hair's shade on the scale of light to dark.*

Darkness Scale:	Warm shades:	Cool shades:
light	very light blond sandy blond	white very light grey
med light	light & dark blond dark blond	ash blond ash blond w/ brown
medium	honey brown strawberry blond	medium grey salt and pepper
medium dark	medium brown reddish brown	dark w/ ash highlights black w/ some grey
dark	dark brownish red dark brown	auburn black

Now, because most of us have hair on about two-thirds of our head, and because most us have hair that's longer than half an inch, *hair color trumps skin tone.* When we're deciding which colors look fabulous on us, we must consider all our inherent colors. However, hair color takes precedence. Your hair color is *your dominant* color and takes precedence when determining which colors are best for you, warm or cool.

Many women have asked me, "What if my hair color changes?" My answer is, "Then your colors change accordingly." If your hair used to be brown and now it's golden blond, your best colors will tend to be lighter and more yellow-based. If you have rosy skin and started coloring your hair an orangey-red, your colors will definitely change from mostly cool to a warmer palette. Your new palette will include more greens, rust, russet, brick tones, and orangey-reds, as opposed to wine, maroon, powder blue, and lavender.

As a general rule, the darker your hair, skin, and eye color, the darker colors you can wear. If your hair color is light, you'll most likely look good in light or soft colors. *The general tone (light to dark) of your hair and skin together equals the general tone (light to dark) of colors that will be a good balance on you.* And, of course, make you look terrific.

But what if you have pale skin with dark hair? We'll discuss that in the next section, "Contrast."

Color is a huge part of our personal appearance, so I really want you to understand why certain colors are terrific on you and others aren't. This next exercise is important, so please don't skip it. You'll need to remove all traces of makeup.

Get that mirror again and go back to natural light during the day. You need to be facing out *toward a window.* Look closely at your clean, makeup-free face in the natural light. Notice all the colors on your face: in your cheeks, on your lips, and on the skin of your jaw and neck. Get creative with your descriptions of colors. Do your lips and cheeks have pink, coral, reddish, or berry tones? Write down all the different shades you find on all parts of your face and neck. Be specific: ivory, pinkish beige, yellowish tan, honey, wheat, coffee with cream, the woodwork in my kitchen, etc.

If you have very light hair and light skin but want to wear a bold or dark color, here's a way to create balance. Let's say you have light blond hair and fair skin, but want to wear an emerald green dress. Simply apply dark green eyeliner or green shadow, earrings, or a green hair ornament. This will balance the volume of color on your body with a touch of the same color above the neck. Use the same principles if you want to wear a navy or black dress, blazer, or slacks. Balance the dark shades that you're wearing on your body with dark eye makeup, sunglasses, headband or hat. That's hot.

_____

_____

_____

_____

Next take a good, long look at your eyes in the natural light. There may be two or three different colors sparkling there that you never noticed before. You may have always thought you had blue eyes, but on closer observation you realize that they're really more of a turquoise or aqua with yellow specks. Write down all the colors you see. Be specific.

_____

_____

_____

Are you wondering why any of this is important? It's because all those colors in your skin, cheeks, lips, hair, and eyes *are colors that will look terrific on you!* Amazing, isn't it! And amazingly simple, too. Plus, there's a whole lot of complementary colors that will also flatter your unique coloring. How do you know which colors they are? Trial and error.

Pull a variety of clothes from your closet in different colors: purple, magenta, orange, yellow, burgundy, red, blue, etc. Bring a stack of T-shirts, sweaters, ties, or pants back to that mirror. If you have no bright colors in your ward-robe, maybe bring a few brightly colored towels. You're back at that mirror now, facing outward toward the natural light. One at a time, hold the items up to your face while looking in the mirror, facing the natural light. How does each color make you look?

If the color makes your eyes sparkle and your skin come to life, then that's a great color for you. Put those colors in pile A. If a certain color makes you suddenly feel dull or drab, if you have the urge to put on some blush, or think you need a vacation... or if the color just doesn't *do* anything for you, put those items in pile B. Be honest about which shades make you look healthy and vibrant, as opposed to sallow, dull, or dingy. Pay close attention; one shade of green might be amazing and the next poison.

Hint: grey doesn't really *flatter* most people. It's a trendy color, and it's sold in all the stores, but it doesn't really *do* much for most of us.

Observe the many shades in pile A, the ones that brighten you up. Are they by chance the colors that you love wearing anyway? When you wear them, do you get compliments?

How about pile B? Aren't they colors you don't care for anyway? Or maybe they're colors that a friend wears, a friend with great taste but completely different coloring. Did you buy those items on sale or because a salesperson told you to? Were they given to you by some well-meaning loved one?

Doesn't matter, because those colors are just not right for you *and now you know it*. Why not make yourself a little promise? From now on, only wear colors that make your skin glow and your eyes sparkle. Colors you feel terrific in, colors that enhance your inner beauty.

CONTRAST

Contrast is important to take into consideration when choosing your most flattering colors. See actress Cate Blanchett on the left? Her light blond hair, blue eyes and ivory skin means that there is a low amount of contrast between the colors of her hair, eyes, and skin. Therefore, she looks lovely in light colors. Jennifer Aniston, center, has golden brown locks and tanned skin. She has a medium amount of contrast. On the right, Catherine Zeta Jones has creamy beige skin, brown eyes and very dark, almost black hair. Her coloring has a high amount of contrast. That's why dark colors work best for her.

Low contrast   Medium contrast   High contrast

Have you noticed that Catherine is usually wearing bold or dark colored dresses whereas Cate's gowns are usually very light cream, beige, or a blush color? Jennifer has warm coloring. She's fantastic in...well, pretty much anything, but especially warm, earthy colors in the middle of the spectrum.

How about you? How much contrast do you have between the color of your hair and the color of your skin? Circle the amount of contrast between your hair color and your skin color.

low   medium low   medium   medium high   high

Here's another one of those too-simple, too-good-to-be-true rules: the amount of contrast between the color of your hair and your skin should be the same amount of contrast in the colors of the clothes you wear. That's what will look the most flattering on you.

Despite spreads in high fashion magazines to the contrary, the only folks who look terrific in black and white are those with very light skin and very dark hair, or very light hair and very dark skin. Or those with both black and white in their hair. Why? Because they have high contrast up top, so when they wear clothes that also have high contrast, they are, in the mind's eye, balanced. In the next chapter, you'll read how, in the human mind, balance equals beauty.

If you've got light skin and light hair, guess which tones you'll look beautiful in? Yes, your colors will be balanced when you wear light shades and colors. You'll look sensational because you'll have a lovely balance, from head to toe.

If you have light skin tone and light hair color, I wouldn't include black in your color palette. Sorry! It's just not a good balance. But if you have very dark hair, wearing black *will* be a good balance for you.

Now I'm not telling you to throw away your black pants and black skirts. We all have them, we all wear them, we all love them. They're slimming, right? But there are many other dark colors that may be more flattering, like navy, plum, forest green, and chocolate brown. The next time you're tempted to pick up a new pair of black slacks, think balance, think color, and try something new. Buy whichever of those colors is closest to the color of your hair, or the shade (meaning light-to-dark) that your hair is.

THE EMOTIONAL IMPACT OF COLOR

You may not realize the profound impact color can have. Think about the packaging on every product you've ever bought — every package of food, health and beauty products, items for your home, even flowers for your garden. Many times, you make choices based, to a large extent, on color. Advertising agencies and marketing firms bank on it. Billions of dollars are spent every year on research and implementation of packaging, all to persuade you to buy their product.

> The color of cement does not compement anyone. Stores often sell clothes in colors they call neutral or khaki, when in reality it's a dirty, dingy, greyish off, off-oatmeal. Check your closet and ditch the cement.

You, too, have the ability to manipulate a subliminal emotional response from other people simply by choosing specific colors. Each color has inherent qualities to affect us. If you live in the city, think about how you feel when you go to a park or to the mountains for some fresh air and a dose of natural beauty. What happens to your mind, your body, your blood pressure, when you're surrounded by lush green landscape, pastel wildflowers, and a bright blue sky? You feel fantastic, don't you?

Think about the last time you had fresh flowers in your kitchen or living room. These days many flowers don't even have a fragrance, so why do we love them? Color! It livens up the room, giving you a sense of vitality and life.

Now think of a cloudy, grey, cold winter day in a city. What are most people wearing? Black or grey, what a downer. Gives you a depressed, heavy feeling, right? And how do you feel when you see a bride in white, or a newborn baby in soft pink or blue? Sweet, tender, precious.

Understanding our response to color and how colors interact is important in choosing wardrobe. Colors help convey the right tone or message, and evoke the desired response from your audience or people you interact with. Colors send nonverbal communication with subliminal messages that can create physical and emotional reactions.

Here's a list of basic colors and their emotional significance:

- Blues: calming, restful, strong, important, peaceful, intelligent
- Creams or beige: approachable, inviting, calming, restful, relaxing
- Yellows: happiness, creativity, joy, cheerful, warmth
- Gold: expensive, extravagance, bright, traditional, warmth
- Browns: earthiness, wholesome, simplicity, friendly, grounded
- Oranges: excitement, energy, warmth, change, inexpensive, fun
- Reds: passion, excitement, love, heat, joy, power, attention
- Greens: peace, nature, imagination, growth, health, environment
- Purples: royal, precious, romantic, interesting, exotic
- Black: anger, fear, conservative, mysterious, sophisticated, sad, aloof
- Pinks: exciting, sweet, nice, romantic, playful, feminine

REAL-LIFE WOMEN (AND MEN!)

We started Marianne's Color, Style, and Wardrobe Consultation at her kitchen table. While I worked on her color chart, her husband Todd quietly watched and listened, leaning on the kitchen cabinets with arms folded.

Todd is an artist who travels nationally giving presentations in front of large audiences. He uses color, shape, line, and focus in his work, so he was intrigued that I used these same terms to discuss his wife's wardrobe. He nodded as he listened and commented that everything I was telling her made sense. It never occurred to him that those same design elements might have anything to do with wardrobe and overall personal image.

Todd left the room and returned when I'd completed Marianne's color chart. While he was gone, she told me, "He's really good with colors, so it will be interesting to hear what he says." I hoped I wouldn't have to defend my color theories to this professional artist in front of his wife, my client. But I believe in color theory and how certain hues can enhance or detract from one's inherent tones. When he returned, Todd picked up the color chart I'd assembled for Marianne. He turned it over and looked at both sides, all thirty-six colors. Then Todd nodded and said, "When can you come back? I want to work with you."

Two weeks later, I returned to work with Todd on his professional image, colors, and, of course, his wardrobe. Months later, he reported that now he notices the color, or the lack thereof, on every speaker at conferences and events. Now he feels like he has top-secret intelligence on creating powerful and positive stage presence. When he's dressed in the colors I selected for him, people are extremely respectful and can't take their eyes off him. He said he feels super confident and knows that his appearance reflects his intentions as an accomplished and influential artist and speaker.

You know the saying, "knowledge is power?" When you use these design principles to express your personal style, you can feel confident, attractive, and empowered to share your most realized self with the rest of the world.

CHAPTER 5

BALANCE EQUALS *Beauty*

As human beings, we seek balance. We're magnetically drawn to it. We look for balance in art, architecture, landscape, and interior design. Our human brain also likes to see balance on the body – on our own body and on other bodies, too. In the hardwiring of our brains, balance equals beauty. So let's talk about how to bring balance to your overall appearance, head to toe.

To create a sense of balance, you need to repeat the colors, texture, and contrast you find above the neck on the rest of the body as well. Color theory was explained in the last chapter and told you how to use colors to create balance, head to toe. You've already learned how to create balance by using different clothing shapes to make your figure appear more balanced like an hourglass. And we've talked about how to use contrast to create balance. Now let's talk texture and scale.

TEXTURE

Most people never consider texture. I'm talking about the amount of texture in your hair and on your face. Is your hair curly, straight, wavy, thick, or fine? Is your face smooth as a baby's bottom or lined and weathered? Curious? Read on.

Imagine an old Irish fisherman with curly grey hair and a weathered, wrinkled, ruddy face. He's got a whole lot of texture in both his hair and his face. On a scale of low to high, I'd categorize his amount of texture as high. That's why he looks great in a thick, nubby cable-knit sweater. It's a classic. That kind of sweater is a good balance for the amount of texture in his hair and face.

What kind of pants did you picture him wearing in your mind? Not silk jammies. Not skinny jeans. He's probably in corduroy or something thick like Carhartts, right? Something that *goes* with the rest of him, to balance out what's going on above his neck.

Now think of a young Japanese woman. She's got very straight black hair and porcelain skin. Smooth hair plus smooth skin equals low amount of texture. That's why she looks so lovely in smooth textures like silk and satin.

The young Japanese woman would look overwhelmed and out of proportion in a thick, cable knit sweater. And the Irish fisherman would certainly look silly and mismatched in a smooth silk or satin shirt, right? Is it starting to make sense?

How about you? Go back to the mirror, in good lighting, and be honest about the amount of texture you have in your hair and on your face. Do you usually blow-dry your hair with a round brush or a straightener so it looks stick straight and smooth? Or do you usually wear your hair curly, wavy, or tousled?

The amount of texture in hair and face *combined* is how you should categorize yourself. For example, if you have smooth skin but very wild, curly hair, then you have a medium to high amount of texture. If you have quite a bit of texture in your face, but your hair is very smooth and straight, you probably have medium to medium/low amount of texture. (And isn't texture a much more appealing word than wrinkles?)

Remember, hair trumps face. So, when evaluating yourself on the texture scale, the texture of your hair has slightly more weight to it than the texture of your face.

Circle the amount of texture you have in your hair and face combined.

low   medium low   medium   medium high   high

Whatever you circled, that is the same amount of texture that should be in your clothes, overall, to have the most flattering effect. That same amount of texture that's in your hair and face, when repeated on your body, will be a good balance for you. Remember; balance equals beauty.

Did you know whatever is lighter or brighter stands out, appearing slightly larger, and whatever is darker seems to recede, appearing slightly smaller? Let's take advantage of this wonderful optical illusion in our quest for balance and beauty. Our eyes are drawn toward the lightest or brightest color in a picture or on the body. That's why I advise wearing a lighter or brighter colored top underneath a darker jacket or cardigan. This will create an organic slimming effect because you'll have a light streak down the center of your body, so the eye will be pulled right to that center line.

PATTERN SCALE

When speaking about pattern scale, I'm referring to the relationship of proper proportion between the size of your body and the size of a pattern you are wearing. I've mentioned this before, but it bears repeating. The size of the print you wear depends on what size person you are. If you are petite, wear small prints. If you are a medium-sized woman, wear medium-sized prints, etc. Think about it. Cute designs and itty-bitty prints look darling on babies and preschoolers because they are very little people. Conversely, prints that are too large for your frame will overwhelm your appearance. You want to look like a beautiful woman in a print, not a print with a woman in there somewhere.

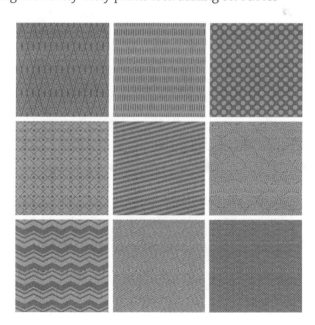

If you have brown or blond hair, your most flattering dark color will be dark brown, not black. Once again, this comes down to balance. Brown will balance your brown or blond hair better than black will.

Matching the color or tone (light to dark) of your pants or skirt to your hair creates terrific balance. Then, if you have blue or green eyes, match the color of your top to the color of your eyes and you will look simply sensational.

This genius technique is understated and subtle, yet so powerful. Try it and you'll get compliments all day. Plus, you'll know the secret recipe to balance your coloring every day of the week. How does that feel? Empowering? You got it, sister

CHAPTER 6

INSPIRATION WITHOUT *Hesitation*

Many women tell me that they don't know where to shop, what to buy, or what to wear for work or even on the weekends. Walking into a department store creates instant overwhelm. They're confused about what to look for, what department to browse, and what to bring into the dressing room.

"How do you know?" these women ask me in complete bewilderment. Sound familiar?

I always suggest making an inspiration board. It helps you hone your tastes in fashion – minus the in-your-face pressure of department stores and eager-for-commission salespeople. Building an inspiration board develops and reveals your own unique blend of personal style.

Assembling a board is really fun. It's not something you do once and then it's done. It's an ongoing process that you add to every month or so. Both the process and the project will give you insight and self-knowledge. It will exercise and stretch your creativity, even if you think you aren't creative or artistic.

I have all of my clients start this exercise before I consult with them. They tell me the experience was very interesting and once they found the right magazines, it was playful, lighthearted, even a bit exciting. You might also use this technique for other projects in your life, like re-decorating, landscaping, or finding a new color to paint your house.

Now, let me talk straight, woman-to-woman. I'm not inviting you to consider the possibility of "maybe someday" creating an inspiration board. I'm strongly recommending you do it *this weekend*. Or better yet, do it today. For anyone who has ever wondered, "What should I buy?" or "How do I put outfits together?" this is your answer. This is how you know.

To make your style board, first get several age-appropriate magazine. They don't necessarily have to be fashion magazines. They can be a mix of some fashion magazines and some lifestyle magazines, but they need to be geared for your general age group. If you are under fifty, you might choose InStyle, Marie Claire, Lucky, Glamour, and even a couple catalogues like J. Crew and Anthropologie. If you are over 50, take a look at Redbook, Real Simple, O, More, and Martha Stewart and catalogues like Coldwater Creek or that perennial classic, Spiegel.

Cut out pictures of outfits, separates, accessories, jewelry, hairstyles, and makeup looks that you love. Doesn't matter if you think you'll never actually buy that particular item. Doesn't matter if your picks cost more than you make in a month. If you think to yourself, "Wow, that is so cool. I love that look. I wish I could wear something kind of like that," cut those pictures out.

Don't stop at a few. Get more magazines and cut out lots of pictures you love. Be bold. Cut out pictures if they make you think, "I'd like to dress like that but I don't know how," or "I wish I could pull that off but I'm just not sure." Be excited by new possibilities you've never considered before. Cut out pictures of looks for different areas of your life: exercise, work, meetings, dates, parties, and interviews.

Get a bulletin board that's at least sixteen-by-twenty inches. You've probably got one in your basement or spare bedroom closet. Hang the bulletin board in or near your closet. It's important that the bulletin board is hanging somewhere where you'll see it regularly. Tack the pictures up on the bulletin board. Add to it monthly and change the pictures seasonally.

Take a look at all the different pictures that you've collected, specifically the pictures of clothes and outfits. What different categories of styles do you see? Natural, casual, traditional, classic, trendy, quirky, whimsical, bohemian, city chic, artsy? Maybe you have your own words to describe the different styles you've chosen.

It's absolutely fine to have many different styles on your board. As long as you love every look, then you know that's a style some part of your personality would like to wear, sometimes. If you have everything from boho to classic Chanel, it just means you like a variety and are not stuck in one certain way of dressing. But if you only have two or three style preferences, that's okay, too. It's not bad or good. It's just a facet of who you are.

Nothing beats having these wardrobe-inspiring pictures where you can see them on a daily basis. My own inspiration board is right behind my desk in my office. Pinterest is great, but that's on your computer or phone; your inspiration board is hanging on the wall in plain sight.

Circle all the different looks you've collected pictures of, and include any descriptive words of your own.

Relaxed	Trendy	Chic
Sexy	Dramatic	Creative
Classic	Feminine	Elegant

Use these looks to inspire you to

- Assemble new outfits in new and creative ways, using what's in your closet right now.

- Style your hair in new and creative ways you love.

- Wear a polished day-makeup face on a regular basis.

- Wear accessories to add pop and pizzazz to your appearance.

- Create a shopping list of what you need and want.

- Shop only in stores and departments that carry styles you love.

- Only buy styles you love, in colors and shapes that flatter you.

- Use your wardrobe as a form of creativity and self-expression.
- Dress to express your inner essence.
- Dress for your dreams.

FEELING TECHY?

Pinterest.com is a perfect place to start a virtual style board, if you are more digital than tactile. Pinterest is an online "bulletin board" where you can create different themed "boards" and pin (or collect) different photos onto those boards from any website.

Create your "style inspiration" board. Then browse popular fashion websites from magazines like Vogue.com and Style.com to your favorite shops like Anthropologie.com and Nordstrom.com. Browse fashion pages in the New York Times. Or Google time periods you feel drawn to or your favorite celebrities.

If you're not sure where to start, simply type "fashion" in the Pinterest search box in the top left corner of the screen. You'll see what other people have pinned and you can repin it onto your board. Consider typing in specific terms, too, like "skirts," "stripes," "artistic style," "jewel tones," or "French fashion."

It's super simple and fun, even if you are not at all technical. Truth be told, it's even a wee bit addictive. Install the "Pin It" bookmark at the top of your web browser. Clear and easy-to-follow directions are available at Pinterest.com. Then, whenever you see a style anywhere online that speaks to you, simply press the "Pin It" button. It will pull the photo up in a different window and allow you to select which of your style boards you want to stash it in. You can also write a personalized description. This is a great place to point out which elements of the photo you like or what about it is perfect for you (color, accessories, overall tone, hair, texture).

Pinterest also saves the original page link where you found the photo. So, in a few weeks, if you decide you want to buy that skirt you pinned from Anthropologie's website, you can click on your pin and it will bring you directly to the page to buy it.

Polyvore.com is also a great site. Check them out and see which one you like, resonate with, or have time for.

The downside is you cannot exactly hang your Pinterest board in or near your closet. If you decide to use the high-tech Pinterest or Polyvore instead of an old-school inspiration board, consider pulling up your pinboard on your iPad or computer while you're putting together outfits. Of course, you can always print out the online images and tack them to your bulletin board.

CHAPTER 7

WHIPPED CREAM AND A *Cherry* ON TOP

In the movie *Steel Magnolias*, the southern character played by Olympia Dukakis declares, "The only thing that separates us from the animals is our ability to accessorize." What a hoot. There's nothing like a great sense of humor.

What can *make* an outfit go from fine to fabulous? Accessories. What gives pop to the plain and sizzle to the sedate? Accessories. What is one of the seven *must-have components* of a polished, put-together look? Girlfriend, you know the answer.

And yet, at my speaking engagements, private consultations, and in my travels around the U.S. – what do I find missing from most women's outfits? Accessories.

We have them, but we don't wear them. What's up with that? When I ask clients why their silky scarves, eye-catching jewels, waist-making belts, or heavenly designer bags sit sad and lonely, unworn in their closets... they tell me they're not quite sure how to wear them.

And yet when I tie a colorful scarf in an interesting and creative way around the neck of that same client, she looks in the mirror and beams, "Wow, I love that!" I've heard it hundreds of times.

British and European women adorn themselves with accessories much more than American women. Not sure why. Even in warm weather, British women wear silk or light-weight scarves to tie an outfit together.

Accessories are the whipped cream and cherry on top of an ice cream sundae – it's just not complete without them. Once you see that for yourself and start having fun accessorizing, you won't stop. To get you going, here are some recommendations on how to use accessories to complete your outfit.

- Own at least five scarves in your color palette, solids and prints. Wrap them around your neck to add interest, pattern, color, and accent to an otherwise plain outfit. Or to camouflage a "textured" neck. And put the focus where you want it; next to your beautiful face.

- Check out YouTube's video, "25 ways to tie a scarf in 4.5 minutes." As of this printing, the URL is http://www.youtube.com/watch?v=5LYAEz777AU. Replay the knots you like, practicing in a mirror until you have the hang.

- Use colorful necklaces, bracelets, and earrings for the same purpose: to add a pop of color, focus, flavor, and accent.

- Wear metal necklaces, fine jewelry, or pearls to lend sophistication and elegance to any outfit. Large pearls, classic pumps, and a French twist hairdo will change a plain outfit from frumpy to fabulous.

- Use accessories as an extension of your personality and to express your personal style. We all need to dress in a variety of styles for different events. Work, dates, hanging out on the weekends and black-tie fundraisers all require different styles of dress. Therefore, you'll need accessories in a variety of styles as well.

- Try donning a colorful pair of shoes to "make" a monochromatic outfit. For a client wearing a beige print jacket and skirt, I found some bright red peep-toe pumps that are now her favorites. I have a pair of show-stopping emerald-green pumps from J.Crew that I use for the same purpose.

- If you want people to notice you across the room and think, "Look at the woman in that amazing necklace," get an interesting, chunky, necklace in colors that go well with your wardrobe, flatter your skin and eyes, and has the same overall artistic flare as what you saw in a magazine and loved.

- Forget about "matchy-matchy." Earrings, necklaces, and bracelets don't need to match, but they should relate to one another. For example, if your necklace is made of wooden beads, your earrings and bracelet do not need to match exactly, but they do need to have some bits of wood in them.

- Stick to one metal. When wearing yellow gold, copper, or silver, stick to it for all of your accessories. For example, if your necklace and earrings are yellow gold, do not wear a belt with a silver buckle or silver bracelet.

- Change your handbag seasonally. The summer bag should be a lighter color than the winter bag. For accessories, choose bold colors in your color palette. For example, your spring/summer bag might be bright yellow or coral, and your winter bag could be dark green or teal. Count the compliments!

- Your bag and your shoes need not match. However, for dressy occasions like a wedding, you'll want a small bag like a clutch that relates to your shoes and outfit. It doesn't have to match, but it does need to have some similarity to your outfit and jacket or coat in terms of style, flavor, attitude, and overall color scheme.

- Try a colorful cashmere pashmina wrap for a more elegant and artistic alternative to a sweater or jacket. Perfect for cool summer nights, overly air-conditioned restaurants, and an eternal touch of class.

- Use your eyeglasses as a fabulous way to make a style statement. Be bold in choosing your frames, even if they are just for reading. Choose a shape and color that flatters your face and expresses your personality. Frames should be changed every three to five years, just like your hairstyle, so your look is current. Just like outdated hairstyles, frames from ten years ago can age you.

- Remember headbands and headscarves. Keep them simple; the colors should relate to and go with the rest of your outfit.

- Dress for business-casual, business-appropriate, and job interviews with a simple rule: eight is enough. For example:

  1. Necklace   4. Watch   7. Ring

  2. Earrings   5. Scarf   8. Bag

  3. Bracelet   6. Belt

- Try Marilyn Monroe's famous trick. After she was completely dressed and had on all of her accessories, she'd take a quick look in the mirror. If any one piece of jewelry stood out, she'd take it off because that meant it was too much.

- Consider Project Runway celebrity stylist Tim Gunn's take on wearing bright, bold accessories. "It's fun. It's fresh."

- Try my little trick for choosing the perfect earrings. When I'm all dressed, I pull two possible pairs of earrings off my earring hanger. Let's say one pair is hanging beads, the other is a pair of gold hoops. I put on one of the hanging beads in one ear and one gold hoop in the other ear. Depending on what look I'm going for, and what the rest of my outfit is, my mirror always shows me a clear winner. Ask yourself what look are you going for and what goes best with the rest of your outfit. Think balance!

- Stand out in the best way. Use accessories that complement, embellish, and pull the rest of what you're wearing together into a balanced, figure-enhancing, face-flattering outfit that you feel fantastic showing up in.

WONDERING WHICH SHOES TO WEAR?

With the rest of my outfit on, I'll put a different shoe on each foot. I stand in front of the full-length mirror with one foot off to the side so it's not visible in the mirror, then I switch feet. That way I can see how the outfit looks with each shoe individually. I ask myself which is the "look" I'm going for. One of the two pair of shoes is always the clear winner.

For even more tips on styling with accessories, visit my blog on my website at www.marianrothschild.com.

Accessories:

- Jewelry: necklaces (chunky, in flattering colors and an assortment of lengths), earrings (casual and dressy, in shapes flattering to your face shape), bracelets (coordinating with, but not necessarily matching your earrings and/or necklace).

- Well-fitting undergarments: bras (professionally fitted), no-line panties, body slimmers, slip

- Watch: comfortable, in a metal and/or leather that complements your skin tone

- Belts (thin and wide, to accentuate your waistline) and a Hip Hugger (mentioned previously)

- Scarves: long but not bulky, in both solid colors and multi-colored prints

- Socks: dark for slacks, white no-see anklets for sneakers at the gym

- Skin-toned ultra-sheer hose (to wear in cold weather when tights just aren't right.)

- Dark tights and/or leggings

- Leather handbag (for cold weather, canvas handbags are acceptable for summer)

- Clutch handbag (for evening or formal occasions)

- Laptop bag or tote

- Sunglasses

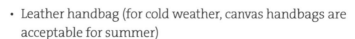

- Reading glasses (in a shape that flatters your face, updated in the last two years)

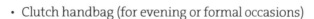

- Gym bag

- Hats: sun hats, winter hats, and visors

- Umbrella

CHAPTER 8

WARDROBE *Essentials*

How long has it been since you cleaned out your closet? I mean really cleaned it out. Are there things in there from the Carter administration? Do you see pictures of beautifully organized closets and think, "Yeah, right, like anyone besides celebrities and talk show hosts actually have a closet *like that!*"

You may find clothes in your drawers and closets you haven't worn for years, and truth be told, you'll never wear them again in this lifetime. We all keep things like that, things we can't seem to get rid of.

"Well, maybe, someday, I might need it for some event where everyone is supposed to wear something from the eighties or when we were in high school." Yeah, that doesn't come up too often.

Maybe you're waiting for certain circumstances, so you can wear your favorites from fifteen years and fifteen pounds ago. Perhaps you're recently divorced, unemployed, or in a new living space. Everybody has things going on. That's understandable. Often these less-than-perfect situations keep us enslaved to old habits and keep us from exercising and eating healthy food, too. Maybe that's why you're holding on to all of those clothes that are one, two, or three sizes too small?

It's great to be optimistic. It's wonderful to be hopeful. It's also practical to be realistic. Being honest with yourself is a form of self-respect. A feeling of liberation and expansion happens when we let go of what's weighing us down.

Try this exercise: Envision your past as a balloon that's been tied to your wrist for years. Inside the balloon are bad experiences or unwanted feelings. Name them, identify them and imagine them inside the balloon, floating around. See the balloon in color, with a string joining it to your wrist. Now take a pair of imaginary scissors and snip that string right off. See the balloon float away into the sky — up, up, so high you can't see it any more. Look at your wrist: no strings attached. You're free. The weight has been lifted, the chains unlocked.

Take a big breath, and on the exhale, relax your shoulders and sit up straight. Feel who you are right now and imagine what you want your life to be like from this day forward. Take another breath in and feel that future you desire deep within your body, the blood pumping through your veins and in your heart. Take a few minutes to write down your dreams for your future.

It's okay to ramble, go out on a limb, let your mind wonder. What do you really want? Write it down *right now*. You can always add more later.

_____

_____

_____

_____

_____

_____

OK, back to focusing on your closet and all those extra things taking up space. Keep the high-quality, well-made classics for when you *do* lose the weight, but not in your everyday closet. For now, store them in another closet in another room, freeing up the space for what you wear now.

In speaking to hundreds of women about their closets, my conversations reveal that women between the ages of eighteen and eighty would rather saw off their arm with a dull blade than clean out their closet and organize it. How about you?

Don't you just love a clean, well-organized refrigerator? Are you the type who cleans out the fridge once or twice a year, perhaps because you don't have a single plastic food container left to store anything in? Aren't you shocked to see all those tin foil bundles hiding in the back, contents unknown? "What is all this stuff?" you wonder.

So out go the mystery-mold containers, the doggie bag from your anniversary dinner three months ago, the ninety-percent-empty bottles of imitation, low fat, partially hydrogenated whatever.

Out goes that limp celery, that watery lettuce, and the potato that qualifies as a science experiment. You wipe down the shelves and the vegetable drawer and replace only the things that you and your family actually eat on a regular basis.

You stand back, admiring the beauty and order of the clean, neatly arranged fridge containing only healthy nourishment. Overwhelmed with awe, you sigh, "Ahh, now I love my refrigerator."

That's how you'll feel about your closet when you remove all the clutter. Cleaning out your closet is not just a recommendation. It's a requirement for achieving the head-to-toe appearance you want. It's non-negotiable.

GETTING STARTED

1. **Label three big boxes: donate, consign, and repair.**

   Rid your closet and dresser drawers of anything you haven't worn in the past two years, except for formal attire, sentimental favorites, and vintage classics. Those things need to be put in a different closet in another room, not your everyday closet. If anything needs buttons, hemming, ironing or cleaning, put those items in the "repair" box. Deal with them this coming weekend.

   If you find relatively new items you just don't like and never wear, put them in the "consign" box. Take them into a consignment shop this coming weekend as well.

   Things that are just plain worn-out, stained, weird, or outdated go in the "donate" box. Fill these boxes. Be honest about what you do and don't ever wear and what you need. The more you purge, the better you'll feel, just like when you clean out the fridge.

Everything that stays in your closet, drawers, and shelves should be clean, odor-free, and wrinkle-free. In other words, everything in your closet needs to be *ready to wear*. So if things need to be washed or ironed, deal with them – yes, by the weekend.

This will be an amazing transformation in your life. You'll be able to wear everything in your closet at a moment's notice. This is an automatic stress reliever.

2. **Next, begin to organize.**
   Hang all dresses together, all blouses together, all pants, jackets, skirts, etc. Fold knit tops and sweaters and put them on shelves within sight of hanging items. Stack or hang by category, then color.

   Shoes need to be visible, facing outward. Special-occasion shoes can be kept in boxes up on a high shelf. All shoes need to be clean, polished, and repaired, with heels in good shape. If the heels of any shoes are worn down, set them by the back door and bring them to the shoe repair *this weekend*, along with whatever needs to go to the tailor for alterations.

   Hang belts, scarves, and jewelry within sight on hooks, nails, jewelry trees, and specially made hangers. Hooks and specialty hangers can be purchased at hardware stores, container stores, closet shops, and even Target. Fun and funky jewelry trees or specialty hangers for earrings and necklaces can be found at shops like Pier One Imports, Anthropologie, and World Market.

   Bags and wraps (pashminas and shawls) should all be visible, or at least reachable, even if they are up high on a shelf.

3. **If you have the space, your out-of-season clothes should be put away in another closet in another room.** This will make dealing with your everyday wardrobe much easier.

Depending on the climate where you live, I suggest moving your winter wardrobe to a spare closet sometime in April or May, and replacing it with your spring/summer wardrobe that's been in storage. Then switch back again to winter clothes in late September or October. There may be some overlap of slacks and lightweight sweaters and jackets that can be worn three seasons, or even year-round.

An absolute must-have in or near every closet is *a full-length mirror*. You can't tell what you look like unless you can see yourself from head to toe. It's just not possible to see your entire body in the bathroom mirror on top of the counter. You have to be able to see the length of your skirt, dress, and pants. It is critical to see your legs and feet so that you can decide what shoes to wear with an outfit. (Shoe choice can completely change the look of an entire outfit from dazzling to drab and vice versa.)

Be sure to stand in front of the full-length mirror after you've dressed. An outfit may look quite different in real life than it did in your head when you planned it. When checking out your look in the mirror, be sure to turn around and look at your backside. You may look fine from the front but there could be a whole 'nother world going on back there!

Another often-overlooked closet necessity is adequate lighting. You must see colors clearly to know if separates go well together. Colors don't have to match exactly. However, you still need good lighting to see the shades and hues. If it's dark in your closet, change that burned-out light bulb, increase the wattage, or try one of those "stick-on" closet lights.

Did you know lighting can affect your mood? More light, better mood. That's important when you're getting ready to go out into the world.

If your closet has a window — lucky you! But be sure direct sunlight isn't beating down on any clothing. Sunlight can fade and discolor your clothes. I know; it's happened to me. Also, the sun's heat can cause elastic to stretch out, turning an elastic waist garment into yards of unusable cloth. This also happened to a favorite skirt of mine. And last but hardly least, never store any clothes in plastic dry-cleaning bags. The plastic emits gases that can discolor and break down the elasticity in stretchy garments.

WHAT TO STOCK IN YOUR CLOSET:
Wardrobe Essentials (per season)

Top ten wardrobe essentials:

1. Great fitting dark dress jeans/jean trousers

2. Knit tops in colors that flatter your skin and eyes

3. Dark brown or black trousers

4. Business-appropriate jackets

5. Cashmere cardigan or pullover sweaters

6. Silk blouses (or silk-looking)

7. Pencil skirts

8. Long cardigan, approximately the same tone (light or dark) as your hair

9. Classic pumps, dark brown, black, and/or nude

10. Comfortable walking shoes, boots, and sandals

Additional stock:

- 1 suit (at least, depending on your type of job or if you are interviewing)

- 2 to 4 pairs of jeans, casual and dark dress jeans

- 4 to 6 pairs of slacks (4 dark, 2 neutral)

- 4 to 6 skirts: knee-length (2 dark, 2 neutral)

- 6 blouses: light, neutral, and accessorizing colors, solids, and prints

- 6 to 8 knit tops: light, neutral, and accessorizing colors, solids, and prints

- 4 to 6 sweaters: 2 cardigans, 2 to 4 pullovers at least

- 2 to 4 jackets, in coordinating colors with pants and skirts

- 3 to 6 dresses: knee length, appropriate for office and other occasions

- 3 to 6 camisoles to wear under blouses, jackets, and sweaters

- 4 to 6 pairs of shoes; 3 pairs of flats, 3 pairs of heels

- 1 to 2 pairs of exercise shoes

- 2 to 4 pairs of boots: flats and heels

- Wool winter coat

- Trench coat

- Exercise clothes

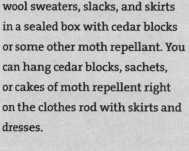

Remember to store cashmere and wool sweaters, slacks, and skirts in a sealed box with cedar blocks or some other moth repellant. You can hang cedar blocks, sachets, or cakes of moth repellent right on the clothes rod with skirts and dresses.

Sachets or cakes of products like No Moth or Moth Away can be placed in boxes or on shelves next to or in between your wool clothing pieces when they are stored for the off-season. These products are available at The Container Store, as well as hardware stores and other locations where household products are sold. Best to take precautions, otherwise, come cold weather you could find lots of tiny holes in your beautiful wool or cashmere

CHAPTER 9

Underneath IT ALL

About eighty percent of women are walking around in the wrong size bra. This startling statistic comes to us via experts in the fashion and clothing industry. Think about it. Have *you* ever had a professional bra fitting? How long ago was that? Are you still wearing the same size bra you wore at eighteen? Um, things change.

Last year I helped a sweet woman in her eighties with her wardrobe and accessories. Now, when you're in your eighties, things are really different in so many ways. Our bodies have gone through big changes by then, understandably. When I mentioned she needed new bras, she said, "No, they're fine. When the elastic around my rib cage stretches too much, I just tighten the shoulder straps."

> *"Having a properly fitting bra is directly connected to a woman's ability to feel best about herself and her body."*
>
> Barbara Wilson, owner of Christina's Lingerie

The band of her bra was riding up close to her shoulder blades, which, of course, made her breasts sag and point downward. That's not the direction we want them headed! Eventually, we got her fitted and into some new bras. Even she admitted that the shape and fit of the new bras looked and felt much better.

As time goes by, our breasts change size, shape, and volume. Sorry girlfriends, it's a fact. The only way to keep the appearance of younger breasts, short of having implants (which I do not recommend), is by wearing the correct size and type of bra for your unique body.

A note about implants: Some women are happy with implants and feel good about their enhanced body. However, I can't recommend them because I've seen bad results: much too large, rock hard, lumpy, nipples in abnormal places, and firm breasts with an otherwise flabby body (which looks unbalanced). But hey, that's just my opinion.

Back to bras! The best way to know the proper bra size and type is to be fitted at a reputable lingerie store or the lingerie section of a good department store. And I don't mean trendy fashion stores that cater to teens and twenty-somethings. Seek out the assistance of a mature, experienced professional. Ask a friend or trusted salesperson for a referral, if possible.

You may be very surprised at the actual size that fits you correctly, if you haven't had a fitting done recently. It's wonderful to have a bra that covers completely – no spillage – and holds you up in all the right ways. When things are pointed in the right direction, your clothes will fit better, you'll look slimmer, shapelier, and you may even be inclined to have better posture. That's *always* a good thing.

Barbara Wilson is the owner of Christina's Lingerie in Boulder, Colorado (www.christinasluxuries.com). I have sent many of my clients to her for expert bra fittings, with outstanding results. Barbara was kind enough to give me an interview loaded with tons of valuable information.

What's the most important thing you'd like to tell women about lingerie?

Every woman needs and deserves a properly fitting bra. Her clothes simply won't fit properly without one. The key element of a woman's wardrobe is a correctly fitting bra. It's a matter of self-esteem. A new bra can transform your shape and uplift your confidence. Women are walking around with headaches, backaches, and shoulder pain, all the result of an ill-fitting bra. It's the closest thing to your body, and you build from there.

What's more important: frilly or functional underwear?

Depends if you're talking about French women. Why are the French so sexy? They focus on passion: love, life, food. The key is getting them both:

frill and function. Women can lose their sexuality if they don't take care of their femininity. It doesn't take much. It's just nice. A good quality bra can accomplish comfort and attractiveness. You can get color, fashion and great style up to G cups.

Why bother with sexy bras and panties? Aren't they only for intimate times?

Sexuality shouldn't be something that you put on the shelf after you're done with your lover. You start to feel dumpy and depressed.

Does shapewear have to be uncomfortable to be beneficial?

Not with today's fabrics. They are lightweight and strong. The Spanx thing is phenomenal; you really do look five pounds thinner. Shapers offer slimming support, giving a great silhouette They camouflage imperfections, slenderizing and smoothing the body without bulging the skin or showing lines.

Your figure, beauty and confidence can be enhanced with the right undergarments. You feel taller and thinner, like when you put on high heels. It changes the way you look at yourself.

What's your favorite brand and type of shapewear?

It changes every day. There's always something new, improved, better. So many brands and choices to solve problems with every shape. You've got to find the right product for the certain problem.

What are your best-selling items in the store?

T-shirt bras; they are a simple solution to everything. They give you a smooth look. But some women need a three-part cup for extra support, uplift, and shape.

The Marie Jo bra is made in Belgium. It's shocking; the difference between this bra and other bras. It's soft, natural, smooth, fits like a million bucks. There are one hundred and fifteen steps to make this bra, that's why it gives superior fit, ultimate comfort, and sophisticated styling. It's designed for active, confident, modern women.

Wow, it sounds amazing. How much is it?

We carry two models; one is $99 and the other is $100. It's like the Ferrari of bras.

What would you like to say about panties, no-line panties, and thongs?

Hanky Panky is the number one thong. Millions have been sold. It's the most comfortable and it just works. La Perla panties are the most prestigious panties. They're made in Italy.

What else would you like to share with women who want to look and feel beautiful?

All women should get a pair of silk pajamas before they die. They truly are the most luxurious thing ever. Sleeping in silk pajamas is like sleeping with a cloud around you. The softer the sleepwear, the better. Eberjey makes Modal; it's soft-like-butter fabric, one hundred percent cotton.

Thank you, Barbara. I want to try all of those little goodies. You gave us so many great tips that I know women will appreciate. Any final words?

Love your bra and feel supported!

This is Marian again, and speaking of Spanx, here's a funny story. At two different presentations, I was talking about the importance of image in business, and why, how, and what to put together and wear for a sharp, smart, professional look. We were working through the subject of dressing to flatter your shape.

After identifying that women want to optimally shoot for an hourglass figure, I wanted to show them how to change the appearance of a triangle-shape figure into an hourglass. I drew the outline of an hourglass on the whiteboard, then drew the outline of a triangle over the hourglass. I explained that to change the appearance of a triangle into an hourglass, you have to build up volume on top and minimize volume on the bottom. You can do this with the use of jackets with strong shoulder seams and wide collars, with scarves draped in a horizontal line around the neck, and by wearing light colors and patterns on the upper half. All of these techniques make the upper half of the body appear larger.

"Then we want to make the bottom half of the body appear smaller. So what's the best way to do that?" I asked the audience. Immediately (in two different presentations), several female voices rang out from different parts of the room, shouting out the word, "Spanx!"

That caught me off guard and we all shared a good laugh.

I'd anticipated someone saying "dark colors." But I do agree that Spanx and other body slimmers can make certain body parts appear smaller and so much more. They beautifully and painlessly smooth out lumps, bumps, and bulges on whatever area of the body they cover.

There are body slimmers for just about every area on a woman's body that may not be the size and shape she would like. Some are just like a panty with special panels in the tummy to hold and flatten it. Some extend down to the mid-thigh area and smooth out the waist, hips, and thighs. There are even shapers that are like short-sleeved shirts to slim the upper arm area, back, and waistline. Wherever your trouble spots are, there's a body slimmer that will hold it in and smooth it out.

Beware of flesh *muffin-ing* out at the point where the body slimmer ends. You want a smooth transition, not a line with a bulge. Look for a style that fits well and feels comfortable. Try several styles and brands to see which ones are right for you.

NO-LINE PANTIES

No VPL! Just don't do it. In case you haven't heard, that stands for visible panty line, the lines created by the bottom of your panties that show right through your pants, skirts, and dresses. They actually outline your rear end, as if there were huge arrows pointing with neon blinking lights, spelling out the words "Look how big my butt is!"

An easy remedy to VPL is thongs or no-line panties. Not everyone likes the feeling of thongs. I'm told you get used to them, kind of like wearing a bra for the first time; you have to get used to the straps. Even though I've tried many brands of thongs, I haven't found one yet that I can tolerate wearing for the entire day. But I'm open, so I'm still looking.

Hands down, my absolute favorite brand of no-line panty is "TC Edge." They have thin rubber lines instead of elastic at the bottom edge, so the panty is held in place on your skin and won't ride up. And you positively do not see the panty line. Heat will eventually break down rubber and elastic, so do not wash these gems in hot water and line dry only.

Other favorite no-line panties, according to friends and clients

When wearing white jeans or slacks, use nude colored, no-line panties or a nude thong to ensure that nothing shows through.

- Felina Lingerie
- Soma Intimates
  (Vanishing Edge is their no-line panty collection)
- OnGossamer
- Hanky Panky (the collection is called BARE Collection)
- Barely There
- Commando
- Jockey (the collection is called No Panty Line Promise Collection)

All of these need to be either hand-washed or machine washed on "delicate." None should go in the dryer. Try any of these no-line panties; they'll be better than having blinking lights, arrows, and lines that highlight the size and shape of your caboose. Silence the shouts; toot your own horn.

At a morning networking event for business professionals, I sat talking with a young woman for about ten minutes. As the event was winding down and it was time to leave, I followed her out the door into the daylight to say our good-byes. As she walked ahead of me out into the sunshine, the light shone brightly through her thin white cotton skirt. To everyone looking in her direction, it appeared that she had suddenly disrobed. Not kidding! You could see right through the skirt material all the way up to her dark colored thong. Talk about sending the wrong message!

Let your personality be transparent, not your clothes. If a skirt or dress doesn't have a lining, wear a slip.

CHAPTER 10

Athletic ENDEAVORS

As time goes by, our bodies change. I know mine has. In my twenties, I was a professional dancer and actress, taking on average four or five dance classes per week. I'd take ballet or jazz technique class during the day and perform in musicals like "Bye Bye Birdie," "Cinderella," and "The Merry Widow" by night. When you're young, you've got energy, vitality, enthusiasm, and *lean muscle mass*.

That was then. Things have changed a bit. I don't dance anymore. I've returned to ballet class numerous times in the past fifteen years, only to quit a few weeks later. My body has told me hundreds of times and in hundreds of ways (aches and pains) that it just isn't capable of moving like that anymore.

But if I do nothing, no exercise at all, um, wow, I become a shape-shifter. Lumps and bumps form in places I didn't even know could change like that. Time and gravity are powerful forces. I'm wondering what I ever did to invite their wrath. I want to stay in good shape – partly out of vanity, I'll admit, partly out of nostalgia for the body that I used to have, and absolutely for good health.

So, I work out on a regular basis. It feels good in many ways. While I'm running or exercising in a cycling, strength, or total-body fitness class, I don't necessarily love every minute. It's hard work. Sometimes it's really hard, depending on the instructor and how I'm feeling that day. But I'm always glad I did it once it's over.

Music, movement, and great workout clothes can make the entire experience of exercising so much more fun. Well, the social aspect, also. I believe all of those elements are related. Here's what I mean. I enjoy being in classes with terrific teachers and great music that inspires me to move. It's always fun being with people you're familiar with and see on a regular basis. And by now you know that I love cute clothes.

I think women who take classes have at least some things in common. We all share certain goals: being healthy, in good shape, and having fun while we're getting there. Cute workout clothes are a bonus.

It's not necessary to have the latest style of leggings and tops for working out or the lightest and brightest shoes designed for your particular activity. However, I do believe those things add tremendously to our motivation. I don't know about you, but I need all the motivation I can get.

That's why I think it's so worth it to spend a few dollars on nice athletic wear. Oh yeah, we've all got pit-stained Ts, decades-old sweatpants, and bargain-basement sneakers we wear cleaning the garage or mowing the lawn. Those clothes are old, worn out, and clunky. And they're not designed for athletic endeavors.

You wouldn't use a hammer to stir a pot of spaghetti sauce nor would you use a wooden spoon to hang a picture. Yet some of us think we can exercise efficiently in clothes and shoes that are meant for yard work or leisure. You can't. You need the right equipment for the job you are doing. And you need the right clothing and gear for the type of exercise you're engaging in.

"When you look good, you feel good. And when you feel good, you perform even better." This is the principle that guided Nicole DeBoom, founder and president of Skirt Sports, a women's athletic wear design firm.

DeBoom was on a training run in 2003 and decided that women shouldn't have to sacrifice femininity for performance. She created the first-ever women's fitness skirt and raced to victory in the 2004 Ironman Wisconsin in her hand-sewn prototype. Nicole pioneered an entirely new product category, and Skirt Sports (www.skirtsports.com) has become a bustling business.

I asked Nicole to explain why dressing appropriately for exercise is important. She had some amazing and brilliant advice for us.

Why should women consider investing in good-quality athletic wear to work out? It's just exercise and the clothes just get sweaty, right?

Athletic clothing is supposed to get sweaty if you're working hard enough!

That's why it's very important to invest in performance clothing that is comfortable, will enhance your workout and will hold up over time. The best sign of a great product is when I don't think about it at all during my workout. That means there are no uncomfortable seams, no chafing issues, and the fabrics wick sweat like they should. On the flipside, if you don't have high-quality performance clothing, you spend time and energy fussing with your outfit – pulling and twisting because it just doesn't feel comfortable.

Why did you invest your time and money in building a business of women's athletic wear?

Fitness is my passion. I've been an athlete since I was six years old on my local swim team, and I later went on to become a professional triathlete. When I was racing, I found that my performance was directly tied to my level of confidence, and my confidence could be influenced by what I decided to wear that day. I started Skirt Sports because I realized that this concept can apply to everyday life, and I felt that maybe I could help inspire women to work out just by creating something cute to wear.

When I had the idea for Skirt Sports, something inside me changed. It was like a spark ignited that day. I knew that I needed to pursue this idea. I also felt that this was the right time to invest in myself, take a chance and follow my heart.

What response have you received from women who wear your products?

My favorite reaction is when a woman says, "I could never wear that. I can't find anything that fits me right, and I know Skirt Sports won't work."

I say, "Why don't you just try it on anyway? What could it hurt?"

Moments later, she glides out of the fitting room with a huge smile and exclaims, "I love it!" It's literally that easy. We are providing a solution for so many women who have struggled to find fitness clothing that looks good and performs well, so when they discover Skirt Sports, they walk away feeling liberated.

What would you like to say to women who either regularly exercise, or are just starting to exercise?

First, no matter when you become an athlete in your life, you will start a journey during which you will become more in tune with your body than you ever imagined. This is a very empowering thing. My first piece of advice is to listen to your body. It will tell you when you are pushing too hard or not pushing hard enough.

If you want to guarantee that you will complete your intended workouts, schedule them into your week. You know yourself. If you're a morning person, get up and do your workout. If you fall into the trap of saying, "I'll do it later in the day," your chances just dropped substantially.

> Evening makeup, large hoops, noisy bracelets, and perfume are not meant for the gym. Save the bling and glamour for after you've showered. The more you look like an athlete, the more likely you will behave like an athlete and the more benefit you'll receive from your workout.

Keep a log. If you know you have to be accountable, even to a simple piece of paper, you will be more likely to maintain consistency.

Switch it up. The key to longevity in life is diversity. Mix up your activities. This will also help your body be more well rounded, increasing your fitness.

Enlist friends or a training group. If you are struggling from a lack of motivation or commitment, find a friend or group who will expect you to show up.

This isn't a short fix; it's a long-term life change. Incorporate fitness into your life in a way that you can sustain for the long-term. If your life is already too full, you will need to do some soul-searching to figure out what you can replace. It doesn't make sense to cram another big initiative into an already overflowing life. Be realistic; it will help you make real change.

I never regret working out. When you're struggling to get your foot out the door, just remember you may regret it if you skip your workout, but the chances of regretting if you actually do the workout are slim to none!

JUST STARTING OUT?

Thanks, Nicole. Marian's back with you now. I've been involved in some form of athletics ever since I can remember. I must have been only four when my beloved grandfather, Poppy, taught me and my sisters how to do headstands against a wall with a pillow under our heads. He also taught us to flip over the bars of the backyard swing set, a trick he called "skin the cat." Soon after that, my older sisters taught me how to do cartwheels and cheerleading in the backyard, after which we'd have running races (Vanessa always won), and play kickball on the street in front of our house. At age six, I started dancing and didn't stop entirely until I was well into my forties.

Now I go to the gym four or five times a week for some class or another: strength, cardio, cycling, Pilates, or yoga. If I can't make it to the gym, I go for a jog or power walk for about forty-five minutes. If I don't exercise regularly, I feel like a slouch, my belly gets soft, my pants are too tight, and I don't feel sexy.

Exercising takes time, but it's worth it. When you exercise on a regular basis your blood circulates, your lungs fill with air, your body is strong and your mind is nimble. Poppy used to tell me, "Honey, don't get old." I know now he meant don't let your body and your mind get out of shape – stay young as long as you can. The best way to do that physically is to eat healthy food and exercise regularly.

There are so many ways to get and stay in shape nowadays. You've got to find what works for you, something you love to do, so you'll do it several times a week. But you have to build up a sweat, breathe heavily, and increase your heart rate for an extended period of time.

Amy Fouchey Reilly is the Personal Training Manager at Colorado Athletic Club in Boulder, Colorado. Amy recommends one hour of strenuous exercise, three to five days a week for optimal results from an exercise regime. However, if you're just starting, ease into your workouts slowly – but not too slowly. She adds, "Group fitness classes are a great way to get your workouts in regularly. You get pushed harder than you would work out on your own, build community, and have fun while getting in shape."

Here are some fun activities to try. Circle two or three you'll try within the next two weeks.

- power walk
- bike
- jog
- hike
- yoga
- Pilates
- join a gym or a YMCA or YWCA
- join a Meetup group for runners or hikers
- indoor cycling
- swim
- cardio classes
- hire a personal trainer
- dance classes: salsa, NIA, Soul Sweat, ballet, tap, jazz, tango
- golf
- tennis

Try a few different activities. See what you enjoy and what keeps you motivated to do it again and again. Join a group, or class, or club so you're invested in the activity financially and socially. Schedule the classes or workouts into your routine so that they become habit – so that it's just what you do regularly. In fact, schedule a couple right now. Get your calendar out, make a couple of dates with yourself, and write in the date, time, and activity here:

Date: _____

Time: _____

Activity: _____

Date: _____

Time: _____

Activity: _____

Call a friend to join you. Who? _____

_____

Walking the dog is better than sitting on the couch. However, dogs have to stop quite often. If they're old, they walk very slowly. I know; I've had dogs for the last twenty years. Dog walking is not really exercising unless you take the dog with you on a fast power walk, jog, or brisk hike. For the most part, exercising is what you do after you've taken the dog for his/her leisurely stroll. It has to be fast. It has to increase your heart rate. It has to be for about an hour. And it absolutely can be enjoyable.

To make it more fun, dress the part. Get yourself a few pieces of quality athletic tops, shorts, pants, bras, and shoes that fit well and are comfortable. Colors? Why not! The latest hi-tech fabrics? Go for it! Athletic tops in breathable fabrics of polyester/spandex or cotton/spandex come in a huge variety of hot colors and supportive or slenderizing designs. Pick styles that flatter your figure and colors you love to wear. Athletic specialty shops carry apparel that's right for your specific activity. Check out stores like lululemon, Lucy, Athletica, Title Nine, and Sports Authority.

If you look like an athlete, you are more likely to feel like an athlete, and therefore chances are you just might act like an athlete. Your cholesterol will be better, your skin, heart, lungs, circulation, and overall health will be better. Your clothes will fit better, which may inspire you to eat healthier. You'll feel better overall and most likely sleep better too. With all of these systems on the upswing, you'll probably be more in touch with your sexuality and enjoy sex more – which could improve romantic relationships. Isn't this sounding sensational? What have you got to lose?

ADVICE FROM A PROFESSIONAL ATHLETE

Some of you may be avid athletes or even competitive in cycling, tennis, running, or another sport. Colleen De Reuck is a four-time Olympic athlete, holder of ten-mile and twenty-kilometer world best times in 1998, and a bronze medalist at World Cross Country Championships in 2002. She was so kind to share a few thoughts on the benefits of wearing quality athletic wear.

"Good-quality athletic clothing makes working out more comfortable. I find there is nothing worse than working out with shorts that ride up my butt or jog bras that cause chafing. Certain brands offer different styles of shorts. For example, longer leg for athletes who like more cover, shorter leg lengths for athletes who prefer a fast and light feel, or with skirts for a more feminine look. Also, the newer tech materials wick sweat away from the body, keeping it cooler.

"Correct clothing is needed for different activities. You will find it easier to run with run tech shirts and jackets than using your ski jacket. In winter, running wearing layers is more comfortable than just one big ski jacket or pair of gloves that won't give you the freedom of movement that is needed.

"I have been running in Nike products for the last seventeen years. They have styles that suit almost every body type. They have jog bras that are more supportive and less supportive, and shorts that have different leg lengths. I enjoy Nike women's active wear. It is comfortable, great fitting, and designed in fashionable styles and colors.

"Have athletic wear that is suited to your athletic activity. Shop at retail stores that offer sound advice for your sport. Go to your local specialty store and get fitted with the correct shoes and clothes for your chosen activity."

REAL-LIFE WOMEN

Aimee Heckel is a fashion and fitness columnist at the Daily Camera newspaper in the fittest city in America: Boulder, Colorado. She takes fitness classes and then writes about them as part of her job! She had this to say about athletic apparel:

My comfort and performance dramatically improved when I discovered what I call magical yoga pants at lululemon. I also found some great, cheaper ones at sports specialty stores.

I believe it's worth it to pay a bit extra for a store that specializes in athletic apparel. The sales associates are trained to fit you in the perfect gear. Also, most of these stores offer free alterations, so you won't be tripping over your long cuffs and twist your ankle. Brands like lululemon also fix broken zippers and snaps for free. Better to have three pairs of yoga pants and three tops that you love than an armoire of stuff that doesn't look and feel good.

Plus, quality clothing lasts longer. You will be wearing and washing these pants more often than you will ever wear and wash other clothes, so they need to hold up. Lululemon guarantees its garments for five years. Consider the cost-to-use ratio: how much something costs divided by how many wearings you'll get out of it. In this case, the higher price point is justified.

Same goes for shoes. I found it invaluable to go to a specialist athletic shoe store and get fitted for shoes that accommodate my own stride patterns and problems. When it comes to exercise, where you'll be challenging your body and pushing it to new levels, having professionally fit shoes is a matter of safety. In some ways, having appropriate clothes and gear is, too. Think about reflective clothing or being distracted on a bike by your loose, flapping shirt. You will feel better, perform better, and want to work out if you choose quality over quantity.

CHAPTER 11

ROCKING YOUR *Ideal* WORK WARDROBE

You've put loads of time, money, and effort into your education and career. When you meet with clients, customers, and colleagues, you want to send the message that *you rock!* Meaning you can do the absolute best job and get it done better than they'd ever hoped. To send that message, image is an important factor. You might have five PhDs, but if your image is subpar, assumptions about your competency may be subpar as well.

When you are in a business situation, your appearance sends an immediate, nonverbal message to everyone who sees you. So ask yourself — what would you like your professional image to say about who you are?

If you'd like to project an intelligent, creative, ambitious, yet approachable image, there are some important guidelines to follow. As Stephen R. Covey suggests in his popular book, *The 7 Habits of Highly Effective People*, begin with the end in mind. Know what message you want to send.

Before you get dressed, give thought to what you'd like to achieve during your workday. How would you like to look, sound, and behave? Begin with the end in mind, just like the architect who draws every detail of a house before the construction crew breaks ground or the contractor hammers one nail. Be the architect of your exquisite image. Plan your professional wardrobe with each piece readily available, so you can intentionally present yourself with *impeccable presence* for any situation.

But what about those big name celebrity speakers who give leadership presentations in sports jerseys and run workshops barefoot? If you're so big and famous you can get away with those signature tricks, go ahead and be quirky. That's part of their trademark, their *shtick*. The rest of us mere mortals need to dress to express our message if we want to be taken seriously in the business world.

Daniel S. Hamermesh, professor of the Foundations of Economics at the University of Texas at Austin, wrote a book titled *"Beauty Pays: Why Attractive People are More Successful."* Hamermesh sites extensive research backing this premise: good-looking people are more likely to be employed, work more productively, earn trust easier, be better liked, marry better-looking spouses, and have the potential to earn up to $230,000 more income over their lifetime than less attractive people.

How do we attain said attractiveness? By paying attention to how we present ourselves: our clothing, hairstyle, makeup, and posture, nonverbal, and verbal communication. We can transform our appearance from mediocre to stunning with attention to detail and paying attention to the necessary elements of personal and professional image

We need to adjust our wardrobe and communication skills depending on our unique role in business. Executives in investment banking, finance, and law need to dress in more formal business-appropriate attire: suits, dresses with jackets, separates with a blouse and jacket, and conservative accessories. For most of us in other fields, business casual is acceptable.

The interpretation of business casual has changed over the years. Unfortunately, many women and men have completely abandoned any sense of personal pride when dressing for work. Office managers tell me that even though their company has a dress code, employees show up in clothes more appropriate for hiking rather than for work. Supervisors are afraid of being accused of sexual harassment, so they don't complain.

Dressing unprofessionally is not good for business and not healthy for self-esteem either. If you dress sloppy, you feel sloppy; your work suffers and you can lose ambition. You might as well have a big old stop sign in front of your desk. I don't want that for you. I want you to grow, build, advance, achieve. I know you can.

Recommendations for business casual attire

- Clean, odor-free, and wrinkle-free garments are a must.
- Clothes must fit well and skim the body, without clinging or drooping.
- Well-fitting, good quality jackets or cardigan sweaters give polished presence.
- Skirts and dresses should be no higher than one and a half inches above the knee.
- Waistline of pants and skirts should be no lower than two inches below the navel.
- Tummy, cleavage and lingerie, *even straps, should stay covered. Completely. At all times.*

- A current, up-to-date hairstyle will add to your up-to-date image.
- Hair should be clean and styled so it's not hanging in your face.
- Polished day makeup is a must, every day. Learn how to apply it.
- Quality over quantity is your new mantra.
- Sparkly, relaxed, or flirty clothes don't belong in the workplace.
- Hard-soled, leather shoes with a back or back strap are best for business.
- Flats are fine with pants, but skirts and dresses need at least a two-inch heel.
- If you aren't able to wear a higher heel because of physical restrictions, a good quality ballerina flat with no strap across the arch can work with a skirt or dress.
- Slouchy sweaters, T-shirts, shorts, or droopy pants are absolutely inappropriate.
- Shoe leather should be close in color to belt and handbag but don't have to match exactly.

Make an inspiration board just for your work wardrobe. Don't use fashion magazines for this exercise; they mostly show you the latest couture. For pictures of fantastic real-life business casual looks, use lifestyle magazines like Real Simple, More, O, Redbook, and Vanity Fair. Also, InStyle (known for their trendy fashion magazines) publishes soft-covered books like "The New Secrets of Style," "Instant Style," and "Ultimate Beauty Secrets." These all have terrific examples of business casual. These books are available at bookstores and online.

- Metals in your eyeglasses, watch, jewelry, belt buckle, buttons should match – all gold or all silver.

- Clothes and shoes don't have to *be* new, but they do have to *look* new.

- Dress as if you are about to meet the most important person in your life, because you just might.

Make the most of what you've got by mixing terrific standout pieces with classics. We call these standouts "wow pieces" or "star pieces." They consist of the absolutely amazing jacket, dress, necklace, or blouse that gives a huge boost to any outfit. What makes an item a "star piece" is fabulous fabric, maybe suede or cashmere, dynamic design (maybe couture), fantastic fit (tailored to your body), and upgraded details like lining or covered buttons. These pieces may cost a bit more than what you usually spend, but it's worth the price for the impact they have.

Lots of women want to know how to express uniqueness and creativity but still look professional without going over the edge. Here are some fun ideas to play with:

- Give a shift dress or other classic outfit some pizzazz by adding a brightly colored scarf tied around the neck in an infinity knot (see Youtube video for tying instructions.)

- Add a thin animal-print belt and nude pumps to an otherwise plain blouse and skirt.

- Update a classic look with a bright, colorful, wide belt and bold necklace.

- Upgrade a straight skirt with a classic sweater, chunky necklace, dark hose, and three-inch ankle boots.

- Add some pop and sizzle to an otherwise classic or tailored outfit with a tribal, trendy, bright, or unique element like a scarf, belt, shoes, necklace or broach.

- Wear one quirky item you really love, like cowboy boots with a skirt, sweater, bandana, and black hose.

- Let your makeup and hairstyle make an interesting statement with a bit of edge, flair, and trend. Think bright red lips, French twist, or hair gel. Look at magazines for inspiration.

- Wear one or two pieces of statement jewelry, perhaps something vintage or ethnic.

Some more tips

Remember that suit you bought a few years ago? If it's no more than five years old, keep it clean and tailored to fit your current size. From time to time, wear the slacks with a blouse or sweater and long necklace or scarf. Wear the jacket as a blazer with dark denim trouser jeans, a nice top (maybe an animal print), and quality accessories. When the bigwigs or important clients are coming in, wear the whole suit with a silk blouse and nice shoes Your polished appearance will make a great impression.

Choose nice-looking, well-fitting slacks in neutral colors that will give you lots of versatility by matching with a variety of tops, sweaters and jackets. The standard dress pants for women are trousers made of fine wool or a polyester blend. They hold their shape, hang nicely, and won't wrinkle. Be sure and check the label for cleaning instructions.

Pant styles for business can be boot-cut with a slight flair, straight cut, and the Audrey Hepburn "cigarette" slacks. Try them all, but now that you know the shapes that work best to balance your figure – you'll only wear the most flattering trousers. Buy work slacks in chocolate brown, tan, camel, navy, eggplant, and black. If you wear your trousers with different blouses, sweaters, jackets, and tops each time, you can create lots of different outfits. Change the look and feel of an outfit by changing shoes from flats to heels and trading a pullover sweater with a trendy belt for a silk blouse and blazer. Don't forget to switch up your necklaces and scarves to create totally different outfits for a variety of occasions and events.

Think quality over quantity when it comes to business attire. It's much better to have a few pieces of good quality clothes rather than lots of inexpensive pieces that look cheap and don't hold up. Less is more, including accessories.

Keep a strand of fashion pearls in a small box in your desk for unexpected meetings or interviews. Fashion pearls are man-made, larger than classic pearls and have a slightly trendy, more updated style. They look great with anything and instantly dress up even the most casual outfit. Also, keep a classy cardigan sweater or jacket at your office for an instant upgrade to your professional appearance (and added warmth when the air conditioner is blasting). Nothing says "I'm here to work" like a smart, well-fitting jacket.

You don't have to wear high heels, but your shoes need structure and support, so leave the flip-flops and strappy sandals for the weekends. All shoes for the office need a back or a back strap for comfort, support, and practicality. A two-inch heel gives a great look, and you can usually wear that height all day without pain, especially if the heel is thick and the shoe is well made. A classic pump is classic for a reason; they are flattering and give a polished impression. And please, I beg of you; no baby-doll flats with a strap across the arch of your foot like a three-year-old toddler wears. You are a grown woman; dress accordingly.

> If a label says "dry clean," it can be machine-washed with cold water in the delicate or hand-wash cycle. However, if the label says "dry clean only," then it must be taken to the dry cleaners. Don't risk washing it.

Every piece of clothing you wear to work should fit your body just right: not too tight that the fabric pulls and buttons bulge, and not too loose that fabric sags. For dresses and all tops, including blouses, sweaters, and jackets, the waistline should be tapered inward unless it's a trendy, current boxy style. It is fine to show the curve of your waist, but absolutely unacceptable to dress sexy or in a revealing manner if you want to be taken seriously. Skirts should be no shorter than one and a half inches above the knee.

Basically, don't wear anything to work that you would wear clubbing on Saturday night, changing motor oil, or playing volleyball on the beach. Find a good tailor to ensure the proper fit of all your business attire. Develop a good relationship with your tailor and insist on proper fit.

Casual Fridays

If your office adheres to "casual Friday," you'll still want to have a professional presence. In other words, nothing you'd wear to clean out your garage or weed your vegetable garden.

Dark wash, trouser-style jeans are polished and professional. But no skinnies, bleached, low-rise, fringed, blinged, ripped or otherwise distressed, lest your employers become distressed as well. Leggings? No, unless you are in a creative field and wear a tunic-length (mid-thigh) top.

Sneakers in the office? Another no. Even if you're on your feet all day or have special restrictions because of foot conditions, there are plenty of comfortable yet beautiful styles of shoes from brands like Cole Haan, Clark's, Ecco, AGL, Jambu, and Donald J. Pliner.

When in doubt about casual Fridays, remember – casual does not mean sloppy; it means smartly relaxed. Business casual still requires a sharp, professional appearance with quality clothes, accessories, and shoes.

Business women I've worked with report they finally feel like it's okay to be feminine at work because they now know how to dress *appropriately*. They've finally found the balance between dressing to feel pretty and dressing to be taken seriously. You *can* have both. Just use some discretion.

WHO IS *YOUR* STYLE ICON?

Who did you write down as your icons in the Personal Style Assessment questionnaire? When I'm working in the Denver area and ask that question, occasionally the name Kathy Sabine comes up. Kathy is the chief meteorologist for Channel 9 News in Denver (www.9news.com). You'll find her giving the weather forecast almost every weekday evening. Along with being talented, witty, stylish, Kathy is extremely generous as well. She gave me a couple hours of her time for an interview.

Have you always had an eye for style?

No, it developed because of my job. When I was young, I was a tomboy — dressed in corduroy and Levi's 501s. When I got my first job on television, I looked at other women in network news positions and tried to dress like they dress. I just watched people I thought looked great and tried to emulate them.

How do you choose outfits to wear on camera?

By being bold and trying things that may be hit or miss. I look for professional attire that's classy and elegant on women in the business, like Jenna Scott, Katie Couric, and Natalie Morales. I watch tapes of myself on television to see what is and isn't working. This is a learned skill. You know that saying, "Dress for the job you want?" I try to put myself out there as elegant, classy, understated, sassy, and fun, while still being professional. I take my job seriously, but have fun and try to be relevant with the times.

How do you not repeat outfits?

I mix and match a lot of things. So I repeat, but it looks different. If I see something I like on someone else, I'm not shy about asking, "Where did you get that?" Sometimes I see something I like in a whole outfit and just take away one element of the outfit. And I try to keep my closet edited and organized. What doesn't get worn goes to the consignment shop.

When you wear skirts or dresses, what do you wear on your legs?

May through November I usually go without hose if I have color on my legs, or I use tanning lotion. Tights are warmer than nude hose, but if you get the right sheer hose with a patent leather pump, that looks very nice.

Why is image important when you're on television?

I want to make sure that the information I'm putting out there is correct: weather, statistics, and advice. So my appearance needs to look professional and not distracting. People aren't going to watch you if it's not a visually pleasing experience. They want to watch attractive people. Although I've never viewed myself as beautiful, more like the girl next door. People can see I'm like them; I'm real and comfortable to watch.

What are your challenges around your television image?

I'm tall, five foot eleven, so fit is a problem. I have suits tailored to fit my proportions. I have to pay attention to things like working out and taking care of your skin, because this is a visual medium. I do my own makeup and hair, which I had to learn. I'm still learning about new products and techniques because we must stay current to be relevant.

What encouraging words do you have for women who would like to look and feel attractive, but are not quite sure how?

Don't be afraid to ask for help. There are people and tools out there to help you put together your look. When you feel beautiful – hair, makeup, clothes – it will change your life. It's about how you think you look – colors to flatter your skin tone, shapes to flatter your body type. There are ways, and it's easy if you know how.

It's hard to be a working mom. I know, I am one. I don't think you can be good at everything, but that's OK. If you can eat right, exercise, and learn how to dress, you can be a confident, strong woman, and that's attractive. That's empowering. Then anything is possible, even things you didn't think could be possible. There's nothing wrong with asking for help. You can change your life in a day.

For even more tips on styling your work wardrobe, visit my blog on my website at www.marianrothschild.com.

CHAPTER 12

UPSTYLE FOR YOUR *Dream* JOB

By the spring of my senior year in high school, I had gotten into the same college my sister attended, and I was eager to leave the nest. But we were a family of seven with modest means, and university tuition was a struggle.

I'd have to work for a year to save money for tuition, just like my sister had two years earlier. Rats, another year at home before freedom. Without many full-time jobs in our small town, I was looking at taking the train into Chicago for job interviews.

My mom took me to the legendary Marshall Fields for my first-job interview suit. At seventeen, I didn't want anything stuffy and conservative. I was afraid my mom would make me wear something gross and queer (in the vernacular of the times). Weren't all suits boring and traditional? Actually, no!

I found something that fit the definition of suit, but with some interesting appeal. The fabric was grey with red checks, and the jacket had an asymmetrical side zipper. My first ever business look worked for me. I did get a job in a downtown Chicago bank as a file clerk in the credit department. Only a couple of people in the office wore a suit on any given day, but you can bet your Jimmy Choos that everyone wore a two-piece suit to their job interview.

You may be thinking, "That was then, things are much more casual now." But even today, if you're a college graduate interviewing for a full-time job in a corporate environment or other professional atmosphere, especially an executive position, you still need to dress to impress. I suggest either a suit or a conservative dress with a jacket for your first interview.

It's smart to research the company before your interview. Take a look at their entire website. Look at photos of executives and pictures of office staff, if there are any. Hang out at the entrance to the office in the morning or late afternoon when people are coming and going to see how they're dressed.

Always dress one or two levels above the position you're going for. If, during the course of the interview process, you notice that everyone in the office or in that work environment is dressed very casually or creatively, take note. When you are called back in for a second or third interview, dress a little less formally, but still be appropriate for an interview. What's appropriate for the job and what's appropriate for the interview are two different appropriates.

If you're interviewing for a position in a creative field like graphic design, website developer, something in the arts, elementary school teacher, or if you're in a rural community, a suit would be overdoing it. Nice separates with a jacket would be fine. Remember the saying, "When in Rome do as the Romans do." Employers want to make sure you'll fit in, be part of the team.

Your overall head-to-toe image, together with posture, energy, verbal, and nonverbal communication, can be the differentiating factors in whether you fade into the sea of job applicants, or stand out above the rest. A Wall Street Journal article by Christina Binkley, **Law Without Suits**, advised on this very topic.

"When it came time to pick a point person for a plum assignment at Manatt, Phelps, and Phillips recently, the New York law firm chose a polished, professional-looking associate over a brilliant and experienced associate who had been counseled, to no avail, to improve his grooming and attire," said Renee Brissette, a partner at the firm.

Maybe you don't live in New York City, where things are a bit more formal than other parts of the country. Speaking at a Colorado Chamber recently about professional image, I asked Kathryn Miles, president of Eetrex Incorporated, for her opinion on image, appearance, and professional attire.

"Interviewing is a brief meeting, and although appearance is not everything, it can be a differentiator between two candidates. When the qualifications are similar, we choose the organized and polished looking person," she said.

Organized and polished – brilliant! That includes posture, clothes, hair, behavior and focus.

Michael Busenhart, a VP at Macerich Corp., states, "You don't modify an interview approach just because you're in a casual town or still in college. Look serious to be taken seriously."

Job interview attire

- A knee-length skirt with a blouse and jacket, a conservative dress, or a pant and jacket suit, the best quality you can afford.

- Clean, styled hair pulled back off the face, and a polished day-makeup face.

- Shoes with a two- or three-inch heel, bare legs (in warm weather only, but not in very conservative industries), opaque, dark, or sheer hose.

- A few good-quality, conservative accessories: watch, necklace, earrings.

- Fresh breath, clean teeth and nails (have a manicure the day prior).

- A leather-bound notebook, copy of your resume, and a nice pen.

A dress rehearsal can help you avoid surprises or even tragedies. Try on your polished, pressed, and carefully selected outfit a few days prior to your interview. If anything is not so polished or pressed, deal with it immediately. Zippers, hooks, hems, heels – make sure they're perfect.

Protect your resume and notebook with a leather briefcase. Wear a watch and check the time. Do yourself a huge favor and arrive early. My son was rejected from an interview because he arrived three minutes late.

Kathryn Miles also says, "It is important for the person to have the basics: clean, ironed, and organized clothing, clean shoes (I prefer them to be polished), a notebook or portfolio with a fresh resume. Other key items are eye contact and ability to organize thoughts. Use of slang is unacceptable and posture is very important."

I always stress good posture and attention to verbal and nonverbal communication. Bad posture can make you look tired, apathetic, and less than enthusiastic. A firm handshake and looking the other person in the eyes while speaking are must-dos. Pay attention to body positions like having your arms folded and nervous tics like leg or foot jiggling, playing with jewelry or hair. What message are you sending?

My friend Angela interviewed for several months, finally landing her dream job as the Director of Research Communications with the Cancer Treatment Centers of America.

"Interviews require suits, even if everyone in the workplace is wearing jeans. Opt for conservatism. People will subliminally judge you on things like ruffly tops, flamboyant or gaudy jewelry. Do a final mirror-check before going into the building."

Additional general tips may seem obvious, but bear repeating: no gum, no eating, cover body art, turn off cell phones and pagers, don't bring a friend or relative. Do smile, shake hands firmly, sit and stand up straight, maintain eye contact and focus.

Changing jobs for more pay and fulfillment, going back to work after raising kids or graduating are all reasons for interviewing for a new position. Just as you have invested in your education, you need to invest in your head-to-toe image. A well-groomed, put-together appearance can lead to confidence, credibility, respect, and even trust. Dress for the job you want. Prepare for the position and the career that you long for with purpose, intention, and consistency.

CHAPTER 13

Shopping IS NOT A FOUR-LETTER WORD

It's a cliché that most men hate shopping and most women love it. Some women hate it as well. Are you one of them? Let's see if we can pinpoint the reasons why. Check the sentiments you relate to.

- [ ] It's exhausting
- [ ] Not sure what I need
- [ ] Not sure where to go
- [ ] The music is too loud
- [ ] The stores are too crowded
- [ ] Not sure what department I need
- [ ] Not sure what looks good
- [ ] Not sure how much to pay
- [ ] Nothing looks good on me
- [ ] Too much merchandise
- [ ] Everything is too expensive
- [ ] Not sure whether to believe the salesperson
- [ ] Not sure if the merchandise is good quality
- [ ] I have to pee and I can't find the ladies' room
- [ ] Too many clothes in my closet now that I don't wear
- [ ] I can never remember where I parked my car

If you've ever experienced any of these thoughts while shopping or even entertaining the idea of shopping, you're not alone. Honest. Many women have experienced some or all of these, at one time or another. Shopping can be a daunting, overwhelming experience – if you go unprepared. From this day forward, you will be prepared. The work you've done in this book has already, for the most part, prepared you.

Before I shop for and with a client, I need lots of information. In order to make the shopping trip efficient and successful, to pull what my client wants and needs, I have to know her lifestyle, what she needs clothes for, what styles she likes, what shapes flatter her figure, her most flattering colors, her budget, her sizes, what's in her closet, what she needs to fill the gaps, and any special concerns regarding fit.

Without all of this information, we'd be in a pickle. Knowing these things enables us to have a shopping trip that solves problems, creates solutions, reduces stress, and saves money.

Let's review your specifics, so you don't waste money on shopping mistakes. The important factors to consider when shopping are: color, style, shape, fit, focus, need, and desire.

Based on the color evaluation you did earlier, write down your most flattering colors here.

_____

_____

_____

_____

Based on your body type evaluation, write down the wardrobe recommendations that will flatter your specific shape.

_____

_____

_____

Based on the pictures you selected for your inspiration board or
Pinterest board, circle all the different styles you'd like to shop for,
including any descriptive words of your own.

Natural	Trendy	Relaxed
Creative	Elegant	Dramatic
Classic	Feminine	Bohemian
Chic	Athletic	Traditional

Other: _____

_____

_____

**Based on what's left in your closet after editing and organizing it, your
most flattering colors and shapes, and what you still need for your
lifestyle and the looks you want, create your shopping list here.**
Check which items you need.

	Need
2 pairs of casual jeans	_____
1 or 2 pair of dress jeans (dark trouser-style)	_____
2 to 6 pair of slacks (same color/tone of your hair)	_____
2 to 4 casual jackets (for indoors)	_____
4 to 6 sweaters (cardigans and pullovers)	_____
6 to10 knit tops	_____
4 to 6 blouses	_____
2 to 4 casual dresses	_____
2 to 5 work dresses	_____
1 to 3 suits	_____
4 casual skirts	_____

4 business casual skirts   _____

1 winter coat   _____

1 casual outdoor jacket   _____

1 trench coat   _____

Comfortable low shoes   _____

Pumps or heels   _____

Sandals   _____

Boots   _____

Updated reading glasses   _____

Jewelry: earrings, necklaces, watch   _____

Colorful, long scarves   _____

Belts of various widths   _____

Non-visible, well-fitting undergarments   _____

Dark socks, ultra sheer hose, dark tights   _____

Leather handbag and briefcase or tote   _____

Additional items, based on the list in Chapter Eight

_____

_____

_____

Before you head out on your shopping trip, be sure to:

- Wear comfortable clothing: easy-to-remove slacks, top, and shoes. Nothing too complicated with lots of buttons and snaps.
- Wear comfortable panties and your best-fitting bra.
- Bring a lightweight pair of heels for trying on with a dress or skirt.
- Bring a water bottle and a small snack, like an energy bar.

- Bring your shopping list.
- Eat before you leave.
- Wear a light jacket. You don't want to be too warm inside the stores.
- Give yourself goals, a reasonable budget, and a time frame.

Now comes the fun part. Familiarize yourself with different department stores, independently owned boutiques, and national chain specialty shops. If you're not familiar with a certain store's merchandise, go online and research what kind of clothing they carry. Take a look at their website and see if it's right for your needs. This will save you a ton of time.

Certain stores are geared toward juniors, meaning the thirteen to nineteen-year-olds; others are for a more mature crowd. Some shops specialize in clothing for career women, others for a more relaxed lifestyle. By looking at the website, the mannequins in the window, or by asking around, you can easily determine the genre and age group different stores cater to, as well as the price point and styles they carry. No sense wasting your time in a store that doesn't carry what you want. No sense dulling your spirit in a store where nothing will fit, either.

> If you shop for cosmetics and/or fragrance in department stores, always ask for samples. Cosmetics and fragrance companies always stock samples to give away to customers. Just ask.

Department stores like Nordstrom, Dillard's, and Macy's, to name a few, have different sections within the entire women's clothing department. These departments have individual names, to differentiate what kinds of clothing they carry, price points, and lifestyle or age range. For example, Nordstrom has Studio 121, Narrative, Savvy, Brass Plum, TBD, and Point of View. They all carry women's apparel and some accessories, but they each have a very different flavor to them. They also have the specialty size departments Petites and Encore.

Don't let these different departments confuse you. Simply look around and get your bearings. Notice if a certain department has the overall style and quality of clothing you want to buy. Ask a salesperson to give you the lay of the land. Ask what age group and what styles the different departments sell. You may rule out one or two of the sections, but keep an open mind. Be thorough in your hunt for treasures.

If you can't find anything you like in the regular departments, you're probably in the wrong department or the wrong store. Or you may need to come back in a couple of weeks when new inventory arrives.

If you are over the age of forty, please do not shop in the junior department. I can't stress this strongly enough. The juniors' section is for teenagers. You are not a junior; you are a grown woman with taste and style. Dressing like your daughter or your kid's babysitter is not age-appropriate; it's goofy. Your clothes should represent who you are now.

Juniors' clothes are not as well made as women's. The fabrics, details, and manufacturing are of lesser quality because teens like trends that are only in fashion for a brief time. "But I like trends, too," I can hear you saying. Okay then, suggestions on how to adapt hot trends for age-appropriate dressing are coming up in Chapter Fourteen.

Pull more things off the racks than you expect to purchase. If you think an item may have potential, pull it. However, don't just take things willy-nilly. Be discriminating with an educated eye, keeping in mind your best colors, your desired styles, your most flattering shapes, and items checked on your shopping list.

> If you've done the work in this book, you won't need the advice of the personal shoppers who work for high-end department stores. Usually they have no special training; they're simply salespeople who've met a certain quota to qualify for the title of personal shopper. At this point, you have more training regarding your personal style than they do! Some stores even go so far as to call them personal stylists. That makes me want to pull my hair out.
>
> From completing the exercises in this book, you now know which colors, shapes, styles, and pieces are right for you. Hip, hip, hooray!

If you have a lot to try on, ask the salesperson if you can have a large dressing room and ask her to check in with you in a few minutes. Use the three-way mirror in the hall, if one is provided, so you can see yourself from different angles. As you try things on, create three separate piles: one for the yeses, one for the maybes, and one for the definite nos. Have the salesperson clear out the nos every time she checks on you.

But before you decide whether or not to spend your hard-earned money on anything, ask yourself three questions in front of the mirror.

1. **Does it fit me?** (Do the shoulder seams line up with your shoulders? Does the waist taper in to show off your womanly figure? Does it pinch or sag? Is the crotch of the pants too low or too high? Is the sleeve length correct? What happens when you sit, or pretend to drive a car?)

2. **Does it flatter me?** (Does the color make your skin glow and your eyes sparkle? Does it flatter your figure? Do you look terrific or at least pretty darn hot?)

3. **Do I love it?** (Is it you on the inside and out? Is this how you want people to see you? Is this the look you want to move your personal style toward? Does this feel like the real you – finally? Does it have the potential to be one of your favorite things?)

If the answer to any of those questions is no, don't buy that item. There are plenty of other items in other stores for you to spend your money on. Don't settle. Not even if it's on sale. Not even if it's a clearance sale. Not even if the saleslady is gasping over it. That goes for clothes, shoes, and accessories.

Your new mantra: I'll only buy what fits me, what flatters me, and what I love, from this day forward.

DIFFERENT KINDS OF STORES MAKE FOR DIFFERENT EXPERIENCES

There is a difference between Nordstrom and Nordstrom Rack. Well, there are many differences. Although some of the clothes sold at The Rack were previously at a regular Nordstrom, that is not the case with all of The Rack's merchandise. Some of it is overstock and out-of-season merchandise, and other items are not nearly the same quality that is usually sold in regular Nordstrom stores. But they are less expensive.

Also, return policies are different for Nordstrom and The Rack. At the former, you have unlimited amount of time to make a return, for any reason, and you don't even need to have your receipt. At The Rack, you have thirty days to return something for a full refund, all tags must still be on the clothes with no signs of wear, and you must have the receipt. Just a heads-up and buyer beware. Always ask about a store's return policy, just so you know.

When shopping for a coat, either a warm winter coat or a lighter trench coat, consider the color of your hair. The only time I recommend a woman buy a black coat is if she has black hair, but even then, why not consider something more exciting like cobalt blue or plum? Brunettes, look for brown, gold, green, blue, or teal. Blondes, I suggest tan, camel, blue, green, yellow, or brown. And for you silver foxes, go for grey, blue, maroon, plum, or navy to beautifully balance your lovely locks.

Sometimes I have clients who can't afford to buy a season's worth of wardrobe at retail prices, but they are sick and tired of a closet full of clothes with nothing to wear. They will have me shop for/with them, and we'll go to consignment stores.

Consignment stores are different from thrift shops. Everything in a thrift shop has been donated and the money taken in goes to a designated charity. Discriminating consignment shops will only take merchandise that is clean, stain-free, odor-free, in good shape, and fairly new (purchased new within the past two or three years). If an item sells, the shop splits the money with the previous owner. Some consignment shops are beautiful, clean, and bright, and display their merchandise just like a chic, high-end boutique. More than one of my clients has walked out of one particular shop with an entire season of clothes for a mere $700. That's shopping smart!

The same guidelines apply wherever you shop. Never buy anything just because it is low-priced or on sale. Don't buy something just because it's $19.99. Examine the item for fabric content, feel, and fit. After one washing, is it going to ball up, pill up, twist up, or shrink up? Save your money and wait until you find something that's wonderful in every way.

SHOPPING FROM THE COMFORT OF HOME OR OFFICE

Online and catalogue shopping have their pros and cons. If you work full time and have a family and a house, it's understandable that you don't have time to shop. You may already know a specific brand or designer fits you well and you want to order online from them. Or if you have a unique body type that makes it difficult to find your size, such as very tall or short, specialty websites may be helpful. In those cases, shopping for clothes, shoes, and accessories online or from catalogues can save you time and effort. I say go for it.

However, scouring the web for business and casual clothes can be tricky and cause more frustration than it's worth. The reasons are aplenty. You cannot feel the fabric or look at the actual shape of the item. You can't try it on. You may not have the same coloring, body shape, or age range as the model who is wearing the item. On her, the dress, shirt, or tunic looks fantastic because she's nineteen years old, five-foot-ten, and standing on a beach in Hawaii with a sunset in the background. Of course it looks great. She'd make a gunny sack look great! That's why she's a model!

Speaking of everything always looking great, fifteen years ago, I ordered clothes from a catalogue my friend Phyllis recommended. Phyllis was a professional ballet dancer with an absolutely stunning body. Needless to say, her shape is not my shape, and she also has different tastes in clothes.

She told me which catalogue she ordered from, and I placed a rather large order. This was years before my training as an image consultant. I had no education in line, shape, balance, proportion, color, focus, and style. I just ordered what I thought looked good on the models.

A week later, the package arrived on my doorstep. I was so excited! But with each item I pulled from the box I thought, "This isn't what I thought it would feel like." "This isn't what I thought it would look like."

What a disappointment. I ended up sending half of the order back and never really loved any of the things I did keep. They just weren't right for me, somehow.

Has that ever happened to you? Do you end up keeping things you've ordered from a website or a catalogue because you so wanted them to be right or because you were too busy to send them back? Catalogue companies are banking on that. Chances are if you're too busy to go shopping in a store, you don't have a lot of extra time to spend in line at the post office.

From this day forward, don't do that. If you must shop from a website or a catalogue, be honest and pragmatic. Only keep the items if they fit well, if they flatter you, if you love the feel and the style of each piece you've paid good money for. If not, pack it up and ship it out.

My last word on shopping pertains to "big box" stores like Costco, Sam's Club and Walmart. In a nutshell, do not buy your clothes at the same place where you purchase your paper products! Remember the mantra, quality over quantity. From this day forward, let that be your guiding force.

CHAPTER 14

THE POWER OF *Put-Together*

Many times I've planned what I'm going to wear to a certain event ahead of time, and in my mind, the outfit looks terrific. The day of the event, I shower, do my hair and makeup, and put on my brilliantly conceived outfit, only to discover those individually fabulous things look horrible together. Even stranger, if I haven't worn a piece in a year or two, I'm shocked and amazed at how it just doesn't fit the way it used to. Hmm, imagine that.

Alas, as time goes by, things may not fit as well or look quite as stylish as they used to. Therefore, make sure that garments fit and go well together *before* you want to wear them, rather than waiting until the last minute.

When you're considering outfits you've never worn before, be prepared to try on the different pieces of the ensemble – clothes, shoes, and accessories – to see how it all looks together. You don't know how it looks or fits until you see everything together on your body. You may need to try on different earrings, shoes, or add a belt or a scarf to get just the look you're after.

Give yourself plenty of time for this exercise. Make it enjoyable; pour yourself a glass of sparkling water or wine, and put on some favorite music to get your creative juices flowing. Lay tops and bottoms out together on the floor or on your bed. Add shoes and accessories. Mix and match combinations you haven't previously worn. Change the blouses for sweaters, the pants for skirts, a scarf for three long necklaces together, and voila, you've got nine "new" outfits!

Every time you assemble a "new" outfit you love, take a photo. Print them out and put them in their own little photo album or save them in a folder on the desktop of your computer labeled "My Look Book." Do this seasonally and add to your Look Book at least twice a year. With this handy tool, you'll never have to wonder what to wear. Just open the album, and there are all of your outfits, already put together!

MARIAN'S RULES FOR PUTTING TOGETHER LOOKS YOU LOVE
(Some of these are redundant, but worth repeating.)

- Use the pictures you've collected and pinned on your inspiration board to assemble new and creative outfits expressing your inner essence and showing the world all your many facets.

- The colors in a printed top and a solid-colored skirt or pair of pants don't have to match exactly. They can be fairly close in color and still look terrific. Same with a blouse and sweater or jacket.

- Update your look frequently with contemporary and current clothes and accessories.

- Look for pieces that add zip, zing, and pop to an otherwise tired outfit. For example, a creative, whimsical, or trendy top can be combined with a classic pencil skirt for instant wow. An animal-print scarf and bright earrings can change a traditional outfit to chic. Try a leather jacket with flared-leg trousers and boots. Add hoop earrings and you've got sizzle!

- When choosing separates to create an outfit, stick with either warm reds going toward orange, **or** cool reds going toward blue. Don't mix orange reds, like tangerine, with bluish reds, like maroon, in one outfit.

- For a slimming effect, wear vertical lines like zippers, stripes, seams, fringes, scarves, and long necklaces.

- Wear accessories that relate to the clothes you're wearing in terms of style, shape, and color. But be bold with your accessories for accent and flare.

- For a current, up-to-date look, wear two prints together if and only if each piece has at least one color that's the same, and one of the prints is much bolder/larger than the other.

- Color combinations to avoid (except during the appropriate holidays) include red and green, black and orange, and the ever patriotic red, white, and blue, unless you are going for a nautical look.

- If you have cool coloring, you will probably look best in silver-toned accessories. If you have warm coloring, especially if your skin has a golden color to it, gold-toned accessories will be the most flattering.

MARIAN'S DEFINITION OF A "PUT-TOGETHER LOOK."

A put-together look is **the sum total of:**

1. A current hairstyle

2. Polished makeup

3. Flattering clothes

4. Interesting accessories

5. Intentional grooming; clean hair, body, teeth, nails, trimmed body hair, eyebrows

6. Good posture

7. A great attitude

Please don't disregard or discount any of these seven components. They are all important and can be a very fun form of self-expression. It may seem like a lot to think about, but just remember how great you feel when you are intentionally polished and put together.

Much of this book is dedicated to numbers three and four in that list. Let's address the other points in my definition of a put-together image.

POSTURE speaks volumes about your self-awareness, confidence, and overall general attitude. Catch your reflection in the mirror or walking past a window sometime. Are your shoulders hiked up by your ears or rolled forward? Does your head jut forward? Is your middle caved inward? If so, take a big breath in and, on the exhale, roll your shoulders back and down. Stand up straight. (Yes, Mom was right.) Imagine your skeleton is hanging from the ceiling by one thin thread. Your head should be directly on top of your neck, which is directly in line with your spine, which is directly over your hips, knees, and ankles. Take another big breath in and feel that alignment of your body. How does that feel?

Get in the habit of checking your posture regularly, while walking, sitting, standing, alone, or with other people. It's free. It's easy. It takes no time at all to take a big breath in and adjust your posture so you are straight, strong, and significant. And ooh, it feels ever so wonderful. And you will look years younger when you sit, stand, and walk with perfect posture. Really.

Let's move on to another of the biggies in life, as well as in style makeovers; **ATTITUDE**. Do you know someone with a bad attitude? Every time you ask her, "How's it going?" she sighs or moans or groans and then complains about the latest unfortunate event in her life.

On Saturday Night Live they called that character Debbie Downer, remember? Don't be that person. It's not healthy mentally or physically. It's pessimistic and annoying. Nothing is perfect. Nobody's life is perfect. Nobody's. But we don't have to go around looking at all the misery and dwelling on the undesirables. Look for the joy. Look on the bright side. Look at what's good in your life now. You'll feel lighter, brighter, happier, and healthier when you project an optimistic point of view. This type of attitude is not being naive, it's not being a "Pollyanna," it's choosing a hopeful life over the alternative.

In her book, "A Return to Love," Marianne Williamson writes, "Events are always in flux. Changes in life are always going to happen; they're part of the human experience. What we can change, however, is how we perceive them."

Accept the beauty within and you'll be able to manifest outer beauty as well. Look for joy and you will have an easier time feeling happy. Help someone in need. Do something for others and you will feel relevant. You are a daughter of the universe with endless potential. Fill your life with goodness, and grace will always be with you. You will feel better, people will be attracted to you, and you'll glow with radiant energy.

Miscellaneous style bits and tips

- Hem trousers and other slacks (besides skinny jeans and leggings) so that they land ¾" from the floor, no matter what shoes you are wearing. Yes, that means your trousers must be hemmed for certain heel heights and they won't be the right length with higher or lower heels.

- Not sure your hairstyle is current or flattering? Ask a trusted friend or someone with a great fashion sense. Look in magazines for pictures of hairstyles you like. Bring those photos to the salon and ask a stylist if they will work for your type of hair.

- Not thrilled with your current stylist? Ask friends their recommendations. Try a new stylist who can liven up your current look.

- Can't wash and style your hair for a couple days? Try dry shampoo and some styling gel. Or stick it in a ponytail, but add a little pizzazz to that pony with a bit of curling iron magic. Maybe backcomb the hair at the crown of your head and add a wave to the front area. Use a cute clip, chic ponytail holder or elastic band that matches your hair color.

- No time or know-how to put on a polished day-makeup face? Well, if you have no time, at least apply some mascara and bright lip color. It gives your face and your spirit a physical and emotional lift. If you have no know-how, have a professional consultation or grab that friend of yours who's a makeup genius.

> When you know you've got an important event, do a dress rehearsal a week to ten days prior. That way, if you need anything tailored, dry-cleaned, repaired, or replaced, you'll have the time without the stress. If the weather is chilly, also decide which coat, jacket, or pashmina you'll wear.

- No time or resources for a mani-pedi? Forget that French manicure but at the very least, file your nails and apply clear polish. Nails should all be the same length as each other. Always keep nails clean and cuticles trimmed. Always.

- Teeth a bit yellow? Have them whitened, even if they aren't as straight as you'd like them. Ask your dentist about whitening treatments or check out those kiosks with laser whitening booths at the mall. There are many whitening products at the grocery store or pharmacy, although the whitening agents in these products are quite weak and may not give you the desired results.

- Want to add a touch of sexiness to a casual outfit? Hoop earrings provide just the right accent. You always want to dress age-appropriate, but there's nothing wrong with touting your femininity. Add a bold color on the lips for an extra pop of trendy chic.

AGE-APPROPRIATE DRESSING

Lots of women over forty tell me they want to look stylish, but at the same time they want to make sure that they are dressing age-appropriately. That's understandable. We've all seen women who shouldn't be wearing sleeveless tops and miniskirts. We cringe when we see a blouse that bulges between the buttons or plunges deep into never-never land at the neckline. Don't you just want to pull them aside and say, "Don't do that, darlin'. That ship sailed a looong time ago."

You have good taste, but maybe you're not sure about that fine line between looking chic, sexy, and going too far. You're not sure what the rules are, how to figure out what's over the line.

When you're in an intimate setting, like a dimly lit bedroom with your lucky fella, go all out for sexiness. However, at work or social occasions on the weekend, even just running to the grocery store, err on the side of restraint. (You never know who you'll run into at the grocery store or anywhere else.) You can dress to express your inner essence – even if you're sure that your inner essence is a goddess – while still implementing great taste and discernment.

Guidelines for age-appropriate dressing

- If you think something is not age-appropriate, it's probably not. Reconsider your choice.

- There's no substitute for good taste. A classic style will always be a lovely choice if you're not sure what other direction to go.

- If you are over the age of forty-five or fifty at the most, do not wear skirts or dresses shorter than one or two inches above the knee, period. Toss those denim minis; they've had their day. Also, consider the idea that sleeveless tops are probably not right for you, unless you work out regularly and have firm upper arms.

- If you are over thirty, do not shop in the junior department. You can find lots of trendy items in the misses departments, even women's, petite, and plus-size departments. Be selective and don't settle for "just okay."

- One animal print at a time is plenty. An entire outfit of any animal or reptile print is too much of a good thing, unless you're going for a very exotic look.

- Any belly that's exposed had better be tan, trim, firm, and under forty.

- A bun or one low ponytail is beautiful for any age woman. Two low braids can look interesting, whimsical, or Bohemian with the right outfit or boots, up until about the age of fifty. Two ponytails (also known as pigtails) look immature, little girlish, and silly on anyone over twenty-five.

- If most of your outfit is classic, it's fun to add one trendy item, like a fringed scarf, hoop earrings, a denim or leather jacket.

- If you have exposed your cleavage, you have invited gawkers. Don't expect people not to look. You put 'em out there, they will be gawked at. Men will lust and women will be put off, no matter what. We call them private parts for a reason.

- Shop for classic, age-appropriate pieces with killer style at Nordstrom, Talbots, Saks, Bloomingdale's, Neiman Marcus, Macy's, and J.C. Penny (but be careful to only buy good quality), and independently owned boutiques in cities. If the better department stores are out of your price range, I recommend designer consignment stores, rather than settling for dull, boring, same-old stuff. See my shopping rules in Chapter Thirteen.

- Two-piece bathing suits, especially bikinis, are best worn by trim, firm bodies that exercise regularly and are less than fifty years young. Tankinis are a great alternative, plus there are lots of slimming one-piece swim suit options.

- If you feel uncomfortable in high heels, or you have a problem balancing on high heels, either the heels are too high or you need to practice wearing them around the house before you wear them out. There's nothing chic about looking like you're walking a high wire or trying to balance on stilts.

- Skirts and dresses are best worn at mid-knee or just at the top of the knee. Miniskirts (two-inches above the knee or shorter) and short dresses are best worn by trim, firm bodies that exercise regularly and are under fifty.

- Short shorts fall into the same category as miniskirts. Mature gals, keep them mid-thigh at the shortest, to just above the knee.

- Do not wear hose with open-toed shoes or sandals. If it's warm enough to wear open-toed shoes or sandals, you don't need hose. If you think your legs need hose, wear close-toed shoes or hose with the toes exposed. Yes, they make them!

- Get a professional bra fitting once every five years. It makes a big difference. See Chapter Nine: Underneath it all.

- Your glasses should fit at the top of your nose, not halfway down. If they

REAL-LIFE WOMEN

A former neighbor, Pam, has clear blue eyes, and always wears bright pink lipstick. I always thought she was chic and sophisticated. She gave the impression of always being cool, calm, and in control. A couple years ago, I learned she was actually suffering from depression. That shocked me. Somehow I associated the boldness of wearing bright pink lips with self-assurance, ease, and confidence. That's the power color has to transform the physical and the emotional, or at least our impression of it, based on appearance.

keep slipping, get them adjusted at the eyeglasses store. Otherwise, they will age you and give you a disheveled appearance.

- Avoid high-maintenance hair, makeup, and clothing and still look great all day with these tips:
  - Get a haircut that's easy to style and don't wash it every day.
  - Have a set makeup routine with tools, products, and techniques that take no more than eight minutes to apply and five minutes to freshen up midday.
  - Wear well-made, comfortable, classic apparel in fabrics that don't wrinkle.
- A dab of translucent powder will take away shine on parts of your face that naturally perspire. Use powder before anyone snaps a photo of that fabulous face. (When I worked with actress Megan Mullally, she would dab on translucent powder during rehearsal breaks.)
- A little bit of back-combing can be a terrific volumizer for hair. But be careful, too much teasing will look dated and messy.
- Add volume to noticeably thinning hair with clip-in, natural hair extensions in a shade that matches your hair color. Buy them at beauty supply shops and ask your hairstylist to teach you how to put them in.
- On the question of whether or not to cover grey, see Andres Mendoza's recommendation in the next section.

That fabulous face

Every woman over eighteen can benefit from a bit of makeup to put back color we had in the prime of our youth at age twelve or thirteen. Put some emphasis on your eyes because that's where people look when they talk to you, and on cheeks and lips for vibrancy. At the very least, I recommend mascara, concealer, lip, and cheek color. Foundation and concealer give your face an all-over even tone. And for a polished look you'll want to add some contouring eye shadow color in the crease of the eyes and fill in the brows if they are thinning and accentuate the brow arches.

Remember I said a full-length mirror is an absolute must in or near your closet? Well, a **magnifying mirror** is an absolute must for applying makeup. The easiest model to use is a wall-mounted, two-sided version with a retracting arm. They are available at most hardware stores and many beauty supply shops. I use mine many times a day for eyebrow tweezing, makeup application, and styling hair with a blow dryer or curling iron. Using a magnifying mirror allows easy application of makeup and helps keep brows well groomed.

Makeup by Sally Walker

For expert advice on cosmetics, I asked my friend Sally Walker to give us her recommendations for a dynamite day face. Originally from Wicklow, Ireland, Sally is a licensed aesthetician, talented makeup artist extraordinaire, and co-owner of Alchemy Mineral Blends, along with Breanna Ortola. Alchemy is highly respected for the quality of its makeup and for the unique and professional look its artists provide. Alchemy Mineral Blends products are available online and in several shops nationwide.

I've seen Sally's work; it's gorgeous. Want to know how to look your best in ten minutes? Sally Walker makes it easy with these simple steps:

Step 1: Brushes and skincare

Besides having quality makeup in your beauty bag, it is just as important to have quality makeup brushes and skin care. Brushes ensure easy application and blending of colors.

After cleansing, prep your face using an all-natural moisturizer suited to your skin type. Healthy, protected, hydrated skin ensures that your concealer and foundation will go on more evenly. Moisturizer also helps the makeup last longer. Whenever you're outside, you also need protection from both UVA and UVB rays with some sort of full-spectrum sunblock.

Step 2. Concealer

Even after a good eight hours of sleep, you still might have some dark or pink tone around your eyes, making you look tired. Consider concealer your new best friend. Regaining a nice even skin tone under the eyes can transform your whole face. Dab the concealer from the inner eye, next to the nose, under the eye, and down below the trough area so it blends into the cheek area, evenly.

Step 3. Foundation

There are so many different foundations on the market; it can be hard finding the right one for you. Loose mineral foundations are versatile and suit most skin types. They go on with a special flat brush in a circular motion for a lovely, smooth coverage. Apply your foundation to the face, neck, and ears to create an all-over even skin tone.

Step 4. Bronzer and blush

Bronzer and blush go hand in hand. They are meant to be worn together. You can wear one without the other but having the two combined can truly transform the face, giving it a beautiful lift.

First start with your bronzer. Our Alchemy pressed bronzer is universal, as it matches most skin tones and is so highly pigmented you only need to lightly dab your brush to the crevices underneath the cheekbones and blend.

Using the plumpest part of your cheek (the apple of your cheek) as your starting point, apply blush in an upward diagonal motion for a maximum of two inches. All colors should blend beautifully with no noticeable start or stopping point.

Step 5. Eyes

There are five basic steps when it comes to applying your eye makeup, but they are all simple. Eye shadow doesn't have to be complicated to achieve a great look that makes your eyes stand out.

1. *Base shadow or primer*
    It is important to start with either a base color or a primer. I like to use a small amount of primer because it helps to smooth the lid and makes the eye shadow last longer throughout the day. Spread over the entire eye area. Or, using a blending eye shadow brush, load a medium-sized brush with a natural, skin-toned color and apply to the eye lid area and up to the brow.

2. *Crease color*
    Use a rounder brush to apply an eye shadow color that is a bit darker,
    like a medium brown, navy, or purple. Starting first with the outer edge,
    work the brush across the crease of your eye and upward, toward, but not
    touching the brow. Then smooth out the edges with your blending brush.
    Build up color until you achieve your desired intensity.

3. *Highlight*
    Using a small blending brush, apply an eye shadow highlight to the inner
    corner of the eye to give your eyes some pop. Dab a small amount of
    highlight on the brow bone under the arch of the brow, helping to define
    the arch.

4. *Liner*
    I like to use a soft color to line the eyes, like soft medium brown, gray, or
    purple. It looks just as dramatic but a lot softer and more natural for an
    everyday look, rather than black.

    Try both a pencil and a brush to apply liner and use whichever is easiest
    for you. Allow the liner pencil or brush to rest on your lash line. Working
    from the inner edge of the eye in soft strokes, draw a line onto the lash
    roots allowing the product to form a line across the entire length of the
    eye. When you come to the end of the lashes on the outside, bring the line
    slightly out and up to lift the eye area.

    Try applying a light brown or flesh-toned liner to the inner eyelid on top
    and bottom. This really wakes up the eye area because it replaces the pink
    with a softer color.

5. *Mascara*
    Accent and define the upper and lower lashes with mascara. Apply two
    coats of mascara to the top lashes and just a few lashes on the bottom
    outer corners to help open the eyes up.

Step 6: Lips

I love to use pinky flesh tones for lip liner that are almost the same color as your lips. When you line with a natural color, it helps define your lips and adds more shape without looking drawn on. I first line the outer lip to the shape I want and lightly fill them in with color. Then I add a soft neutral pink toned gloss such as Alchemy's Loveland or Chicory gloss.

For more on Sally, Bre, and Alchemy Mineral Blends products, visit alchemymineralblends.com.

HAIR CARE SUGGESTIONS FROM A MASTER STYLIST

Andres Mendoza started doing hair in 1997 at the early age of seventeen. Now he is an educator for Sebastian Professional, Wella Professionals, and Ion Color Brilliance. He recently joined with partners at the Side Door Salon in Boulder, Colorado, where he is the hot, young, go-to stylist in town. Women (who sometimes wait eight to ten weeks for an appointment) adore him, and other stylists admire and respect him. He was nice enough to give us this advice.

When women go to their hairstylist, what should they be equipped with? What should they communicate to their stylist to make sure they will be satisfied with their hair?

Their lifestyle. If the stylist gives a woman something that isn't functional or isn't their personality, it won't work. Tell the stylist your daily routine: how much time you have to do your hair, what you do for a living, profession, artistic endeavors, characteristics, daily activities, how active you are. Then say to your stylist, "Please make my hairstyle work with all those things."

What basic fundamentals should every woman know about hair care?

Know which shampoo is best for your type of hair. Use the correct conditioner for your type of hair. Avoid generic products; they can contain too much alcohol and preservatives that coat your hair. Your stylist should inform you which products and styling tools to use. If your stylist doesn't volunteer this information, ask him or her. If the stylist doesn't know, find another stylist.

How often should we wash our hair?

If it gets dried out, you might be over-washing it. If you have oiliness, you might be over-washing it. Do not wash it every day, at the most every other day, maybe every three or four days. The oils are good for your hair. Depends on lifestyle, also. Even if you work out every day and your hair gets sweaty, just rinse rather than shampoo your hair.

Many women have a very difficult time blow-drying their hair. It never looks like it did when we left the salon. Please advise us on blow-drying.

Practice makes perfect. Keep asking your stylist for instructions and watch YouTube tutorial videos. Blow-drying takes a while to learn. There's a learning curve for dexterity, muscle fatigue, and holding the brush over your head. Make it a bi-weekly routine. Start with once a week, then twice a week. If it ends up being burdensome, you are more likely not to do it. Practice, even if you're not going out. You can always rinse it out if it doesn't work.

What other ways of curling or straightening hair should women familiarize themselves with?

Wet sets are really good; wrapping with rollers or pins when it's semi-wet. Also upstyling, like bubble buns and chignons, can be nice to add wave to the hair. Braiding the hair when slightly wet and then letting it down can be a really interesting look, kind of Bohemian.

To learn those techniques, look up tutorials on the Internet and YouTube. Some stylists and product brands post tutorials on blogs, websites, and Youtube. You are not alone. There is a lot of help out there.

What are three of the most common mistakes that women make regarding their hair?

1. A lot of women assume they have a round face. That may not be the case. Ask the stylist for a cut that flatters your face shape, and accentuates your best feature.

2. Women forget to pay attention to their profile. They may look good from the front in a certain hairstyle, but it may not look good from the side. So they should use another mirror to see themselves from different angles. For example, a high bun may emphasize a large nose or loose skin under the chin. In those cases, a low bun is better.

3. Over-styling: using a curling iron or flat iron every day, or hot rollers every day. If you use heat on your hair every day, the integrity of the hair is lost. It can lose its shine and luster.

What's your take on covering grey?

There is a point where grey is fine for your skin tone; if you have dark golden skin, grey hair looks great. But if you have light rosy skin tone, grey can make your skin look dull and sallow. I would add some of her original hair color or add a glaze, which is a semi-permanent color, or completely cover the grey by changing the all-over color in general.

What's your advice on choosing color?

The more you stray from your natural hair color, the more time you add to the amount of maintenance for your hair care routine. Changing the color too much will harm the integrity of the hair. So consider the health of the hair.

To try out a new color, go to a wig shop and try on a few different colors and styles. You have to feel comfortable with the colors. Definitely you want to have images of what you want and don't want. Bring in photos from magazines of colors and styles that you like. Ask the stylist if it's possible and if they have enough time to accomplish the results you want. Check for timing because if the stylist doesn't have enough time to do your cut and color the way you want it, you may not be happy.

Generally speaking, if you have pink skin or cool coloring, your highlights should be wheat-colored or more of an ashy tone. Stay away from anything brassy or bronze. But if you have warm skin like golden, then golden highlights look good, kind of a honey color looks nice.

What else would you like to tell women about hair?

Hair is such a personal thing. You need to know what you like and what you want. Have lots of one-on-one interaction with your stylist so he or she can use the shape of your head and face. Don't be discouraged if a new style doesn't turn out, because your hair will grow out. Work with it and let it do what it wants to do. Don't try to force your hair to do something that's completely unnatural. If something doesn't work, I reassess and try something different.

Time is always a big factor for women getting ready for their day or for an event. They don't have a lot of time to do their hair. Your advice?

If you don't have time to do your hair and get yourself ready for work or social situations, check with your lifestyle; something may need adjusting. Invest in your appearance. That's how we interact with society when we are out and about – with our appearance. All the women I've known want to look nice, you know? So take the time that you need to ensure that happens.

Andres gave me these hairstyle recommendations for different face shapes.

Face shape: OVAL

Hairstyle recommendations: many choices

As its name implies, the oval-shaped face is longer than wide, with a jaw that's narrower than the cheekbones. Because the oval shaped face has no dominant areas and is so proportional, this face looks good with just about any hairstyle, length or texture. Lucky you!

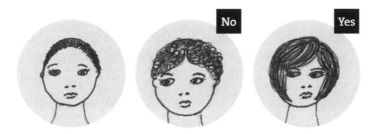

Face shape: ROUND

Hairstyle recommendations: avoid width

The round-shaped face is characterized by a wide hairline and fullness below the cheekbones. You may be overweight and the neck may appear short. These faces look good with geometric or linear styles. Add height, when possible, and long wispy side areas to make the cheeks look narrow. Comb hair close to the head on the side and at the nape.

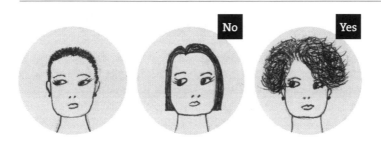

Face shape: SQUARE

Hairstyle recommendations: Avoid straight lines

A square-shaped face is characterized by a wide hairline and jaw. Square-shaped faces need height on top and narrowness at the sides. Comb the hair off the forehead to add height to the face. Curly texture and wisps of hair around the face break the wide, straight lines common to the square line.

Face shape: DIAMOND

Hairstyle recommendations: Reduce width at side

The diamond-shaped face is characterized by a narrow chin and forehead with wide cheekbones. Diamond-shaped faces need narrow sides and fullness at the chin. Bobs work very well for this shape. Avoid wearing height on top or volume on the sides. Use some fringe or bangs to cover narrow forehead.

Face shape: HEART

Hairstyle recommendations: Add volume at chin

The heart-shaped face is characterized by a wider forehead and a narrower chin. Bring some hair onto the forehead to disguise its width. Keep hair close to the head at the eyes but make it slightly full around the jaw and below and in front of the earlobes.

Face shape: PEAR

Hairstyle recommendations: Add volume above jaw line

The pear-shaped face is characterized by a small or narrow forehead and a rather large pouchy-appearing jawline. Layer hair on top of head to add width from eye level through the crown. Set and comb hair close to the head on the side and at the nape.

Face shape: OBLONG

Hairstyle recommendations: Add softness

The oblong-shaped face is characterized by a long and narrow bone structure. If you have an oblong face shape, you often have a long, thin neck. Use a fringe or half-bang across the forehead by creating soft waves or curls in the crown and nape areas. This helps to create the illusion of an oval.

Andres styles hair at The Side Door Salon. That website is www.thesidedoorsalon.com.

PACKING FOR VACATION AND BUSINESS

I love to go on vacation with my sisters. Both of them are silly, witty, and wise. Although we each live in different parts of the country now, we usually get along terrifically, enjoy many of the same activities, and have very similar tastes. All three of us love cooking, strolling on a beach, discussing books, relationships, and gardening.

Both of my sisters are excellent and creative cooks, a trait we inherited from my father. Whenever we can, we shop farmers' markets, oohing and ahhing at all the beautiful produce and sharing ideas for succulent dishes. Then in the evening, inevitably we'll be in the kitchen cooking, chatting, drinking wine, and singing along with oldies songs on the radio from the sixties and seventies, ad-libbing choreography, and inserting jokes.

My oldest sister, Kathy, taught me how to shop economically, roll my hair in curlers, and apply makeup, taking at least double the usual amount of time for special occasions like prom. Kathy is a natural beauty with great features, long dark hair, and a great sense of style. In fact, she's the one whose great clothes I'd sneak out of the house wearing on my way to junior high.

On one of our sibling vacations, I shared a hotel room with Kathy. We were visiting our other sister Vanessa on the California coast. Although we were only staying for three nights, Kathy brought a huge suitcase, big enough to hold two weeks' worth of travel necessities. It was full of clothes, shoes, hair-styling electronics, and toiletries.

When I asked her why she brought so much, she said, "Well, I wasn't sure what the weather was going to be like and where we were going for dinner, so I didn't know what I would want to wear. So I just brought a bunch of choices. And I'd have to wear different shoes depending on what outfit I decided to wear, so that's why I have five pair of shoes."

Now, Kathy may have taught me a lot of things, but vacation packing wasn't one of them. To me it seems unnecessary to lug around a huge suitcase full of all sorts of paraphernalia for a weekend visit with family. Especially since we now have online weather forecasts literally at our fingertips.

Both Kathy and Vanessa were my role models in many respects. Vanessa was always very active, outgoing, and organized. Even now she religiously hits the treadmill and yoga studio, works full-time, and is extremely pragmatic and sensible. She's all about productivity and efficiency. I like to think that I have some of each of their strengths. So, as a tribute to my beloved sisters, I decided to include this bit on efficient fashion – or fashionable efficiency while traveling.

TIPS FOR PACKING

- The day before you leave, Google the weather for the city or area you're traveling to. That will tell you what type of jacket, sweaters, shoes, and rain gear you'll need.

- Wear your bulkiest shoes, pants, sweaters, and jackets on the plane. If possible, pack a heavy coat instead of carrying it onboard.

- Pack heavy items, such as shoes, first on the bottom layer of your suitcase.

- Utilize the zippered expandable option on your luggage to pack folded pants and other flat items.

- Wrap tissue paper or plastic bags from the dry-cleaners around items you wish to remain wrinkle-free.

- Roll sweaters, knit tops, T-shirts and other cotton items. Pack only your most wrinkle-resistant clothing.

- Color-coordinate clothes so everything can be mixed and matched. Try to avoid bringing all black, unless you're traveling for a memorial service.

- If you'll be staying someplace with shampoo, conditioner, and lotion, don't pack those items.

- Consider how many days you will be gone. That's how many pair of undies and how many tops you'll need.

- You can always hand-wash small items in the sink, squeeze, and hang to dry.

- Women have a tendency to overpack. Be honest; only take what you'll truly need, plus a lightweight hostess gift.

For even more tips on styling your put-together look visit my blog on my website at www.marianrothschild.com.

CHAPTER 15

DRESS FOR YOUR *Dreams*

When I was eighteen, before I could go away to college, I had to work for a year to earn a good chunk of my tuition. Coming from a modest-means family, the middle of five children, if we wanted to go away to college, we each had to contribute to our college fund, big time. Therefore, I worked for eleven months at Central National Bank in downtown Chicago.

I mentioned applying for a college scholarship through the pageant system while working at the bank. One morning after sending in my application, I got a phone call at work, from the scholarship committee chairman. He invited me to lunch to discuss my application. He was going to be downtown on business, so it had to be that day. Must go to lunch, must impress!

As I hung up the phone, I looked down at myself and was struck with the feeling of disaster. I was wearing a denim sundress, a ponytail, bare legs, and Dr. Scholl's wooden flip-flop sandals. Remember those? Pretty darn casual, not even remotely business attire, and not an impressive image, even for an informational meeting.

I was about to meet with someone who could provide my golden ticket, a means of reaching my goal, achieving my dream of going away to college. And I looked like I was going for a stroll on the beach. Which can be a cute look, but not for an interview meeting.

A typical hysterical teenager, I called my mother.

Of course, Mom was thrilled to hear about the meeting. She explained the importance of expressing myself clearly, speaking well, and displaying good table manners during lunch. It was very important, she advised, to make sure this decision-maker understood I was worthy of his organization's financial support. Therefore, I had to make the best impression in every possible way.

"I know, I know," I kept repeating. She finally detected a quiver in my voice on my third "I know," as I looked down at my overly casual attire.

"Marian, what's the matter? You'll do fine."

"It's not that." With a furrowed brow, I took a big inhale and an audible exhale. I explained what I'd worn to work that day.

She knew I felt bad. She also knew, in her motherly wisdom, that berating me for not being prepared for any possible situation wouldn't help matters. She knew what we needed was a solution, fast. She provided one. Before I hung up the phone, I added gratefully, "Thanks, Mom."

I ended up borrowing a jacket from Ann the secretary, a pearl necklace from Rose who sat up front, and two-inch heels (a little too small) from Deb who sat in the back. Then I had to run to the corner drugstore for pantyhose because in those days, you had to have nylons for a polished, professional look. I had to duck in the restroom to put them on. And then I had to run the two blocks over to the restaurant in the Midwest humidity.

I arrived at the lunch meeting sweaty, eight minutes late, and thoroughly flustered. My mind was extremely distracted, when I needed to be laser focused.

Here's what I learned. Being caught off guard, unprepared, and inappropriate, even for a surprise situation, was a huge stress. Unexpected things come up — that's just life — and it feels *much* better to be prepared than to be panicked. What I learned was, dress for your dreams. In my case that meant a small but much needed scholarship to help me fund my college education. Got it!

Dress for your dreams. Your dream job, your dream date, your dream mate!

What about you? Has anything like that ever happened to you? You're sitting at home working on your laptop in your sweats and sneakers, haven't showered. It occurs to you that you need to go to the grocery store to get something for dinner. You think, "Oh, It's *just* the grocery store." So you hurry over to the deli counter – and who's standing there? Your ex. And he's with someone.

Or maybe it's time for your regular department meeting or networking group and you think, "Oh, it's just the same old people as always, they all know me." You arrive, and doggone it, there's somebody new there that week. Of course it's somebody who could be an amazing contact for your career, or maybe it's someone whom you'd just like to see again.

Dress for your dreams: your dream client, your dream career, your dream destination!

How does that phrase apply to *you*? What does it mean deep inside your soul? Where does it *get* you? Where could it *take* you? Write whatever occurs to you as an answer to those last four questions. Take your time. Add to it whenever something else occurs to you.

_____

_____

_____

_____

Your appearance is your visual signature, the image that everyone sees; it's your personal logo. Dr. Michio Kaku, a theoretical physicist, says a huge chunk of our brain is devoted to processing visual images. "It's how we communicate. It's by images that we understand the universe," Kaku says.

How valuable will it be to your career and your personal life to only wear colors that make your eyes sparkle and your skin glow, to only wear shapes that flatter your unique figure, and styles that you love? How much stress will be avoided by having your closet edited and organized, by purchasing and wearing only clothing that fits, that makes you look and feel fantastic? How much time will you save getting dressed and how much pressure will be relieved by not having to wonder about your attire for any situation? How much more joyful will your life be when you feel confident, attractive, and genuine for every occasion? When you are that confident person, you'll be capable of making that contribution to the world only you can give.

Polish your presence by giving *exquisite intention, direction, and consistency* to every choice concerning your head-to-toe, inside and out, personal image.

Sizzle your style.

Dress for your dreams.

Don't wait.

Look good now.

ABOUT THE AUTHOR

Marian Rothschild, AICI FLC, is a Certified Personal Image Consultant, founder and president of Look Good Now. A former actress, dancer, and model, Marian and her husband have two sons and live in Colorado. She is a dog owner, organic gardener, and avid athlete on a quest to lead a healthy, balanced, and joyful life.

Please visit www.marianrothschild.com.